Doctors in an Information Technology Age

George O. Obikoya

Table of Contents

Executive Summary

The gap between a vision of healthcare delivery that guarantees access to qualitative healthcare for all and reality in many countries across the globe attests to the complexity of the issues involved in contemporary healthcare delivery on which its transition to the future hinges. It also indicates the need for urgent action to address these issues if we were to eliminate the gap. That doctors are key players in any initiative to do so is not in question and some indeed, would attribute the reasons for the gap, at least in part, to the seeming disinclination of doctors and the health industry as a whole to embrace healthcare information and communication technologies.

This book emphasizes the need for doctors and other healthcare professionals to lead the efforts to promote the widespread diffusion of these technologies in the health industry, in both the clinical and non-clinical domains. It explores the mechanisms underlying the interaction of issues germane to healthcare delivery in both domains and the central role that doctors could play, managing the mechanisms in achieving this crucial, and indeed, historical role in the future of healthcare delivery.

It seems plausible that more effective policing of such laws as the federal Health Insurance Portability and Accountability Act (HIPAA) in the United States would inspire compliance by the health industry with its requirements for technological upgrades for a streamlined, more efficient claims processing simultaneously assuring privacy protection, for example. It might also be such that an appeal to virtue would rouse action from within independent of external encumbrances to prevent the inevitable disease burden on society that the lack of access to qualitative healthcare by many engenders. Regardless, the need for action in many health systems worldwide with healthcare spending soaring relentlessly, in many cases with little to show for it in the quality of health services provision is no doubt rife, and doctors need to be at its vanguard, as this book argues.

The evolution of healthcare delivery and progress in the technologies that have the potential to ensure not just its ability to achieve the dual healthcare goals of being qualitative and at once cost-effective, but also to spawn innovative models of care that would in turn stimulate interest in technological value creation, in a continuous, essentially symbiotic dyadic, are intertwined. The involvement of doctors in these processes seems likely to increase, as the very future of healthcare delivery, which in many countries is in a precarious balance unfolds, doctors the pivot.

Introduction

Doctors are major players in the healthcare delivery arena in a multi-trillion dollar industry in the United States alone. Yet, many question their commitment to helping this industry solve the twin problems of ever-increasing costs and healthcare consumers equally mounting demand for qualitative health services it faces. The reason for this query is not far to seek, considering the legendary seemingly laid -back attitude of doctors toward the healthcare information and communication technologies that could facilitate the achievement of the dual healthcare delivery objectives of qualitative yet cost-effective health services provision that would essentially nullify these twin problems. However, it appears increasingly, that this image of doctors vis-à-vis healthcare information and communication technologies, need a radical makeover. For one, doctors have a crucial obligation to honour, that of not doing harm to their patients, which translates to doing good as doing nothing could result in harm. This is an important ethico-moral dilemma that doctors would face if they continued to turn their backs, literally, to these technologies, which no doubt have a major role to play in not just improving the quality of care that they deliver to their patients, but also in doing so efficiently and cost-effectively. These latter attributes create a different set of dilemmas for doctors that range from questions regarding their commitments to ensuring the survival of the health systems in which they operate to even that of their country at large. There also are the potential legal challenges they might face not complying, for example in the U.S., with the provisions of the Health Insurance Portability and Accountability Act (HIPAA), among others. It is clear therefore that doctors, and indeed, other healthcare professionals would have to reconsider their stand on these technologies and start to embrace, implement, and utilize them for the betterment of the entire healthcare delivery enterprise.

In this book, we will explore in-depth some of the issues underlying the delivery of health services, and indeed, required for im proving them to meet the increasingly suave demands of the contemporary healthcare consumer. We will examine, among others, why today s doctors cannot continue to rely on intermediaries for examples, clearinghouses, and billing agencies, to take care of their reimbursement claims. We will also examine more clinical-related issues for example why a patient slipping into coma should have to wait for an ER doctor trying to reach the patient s GP on the phone to find out potentially life-saving patient information, even then not able to speak with the GP, the patient eventually dying. These and other issues, for examples, those concerning the privacy and confidentiality of patient information, and even the technical, political, and socio-economic dimensions of the implementation and use of healthcare ICT in healthcare delivery, constitute the subject-matter of this book.

At the end of it all, we would have been able to tease out the dynamics of the progress of healthcare delivery and that of these technologies, and the pivotal role that doctors play in the success of this dyadic, which is of major significance in the achievement of the dual healthcare delivery goals.

Doctors, Computers, and the Future of Healthcare Delivery

Healthcare delivery is in turmoil in many countries, and some blame doctors at least in part for it. Soaring healthcare costs, lack of or limited access to health services, increasing patient dissatisfaction with their care, concerns about information privacy and security, increasing rates of medical errors, some potentially fatal, skewed care quality, even charges of misdemeanour against some doctors, are among the many problems that plague contemporary health systems, and for which many hold doctors partly accountable. Meanwhile doctors too have their grudges with the health system, many discontented due to overwork, too little recompense, fear of litigation, even loss of job or status, these issues and many more of such concern increasingly fewer medical students are opting for certain specialties. These issues underscore the significance of health to the healthcare consumer, but belie that to the provider, who in fact had sworn to do no harm to the former under any circumstances. In other words, barring the archetypal exception to every rule, literally, it is difficult to see how doctors would deliberately work against their patients interests, and indeed, those of the health system at large, although this does not mean that certain actions or inactions attributable to doctors could not result inadvertently in negative consequences for either or both. Our focus should be on determining what such actions are, their origins, and what we could do to prevent them happening again, thereby, eventually improving the quality of healthcare delivery in keeping with the aspirations of all healthcare stakeholders. These aspirations, which expectedly differ in details with stakeholders, of course converge, and in summary amount to the delivery of qualitative health services, cost-effectively, what we could term, the achievement of the dual healthcare delivery objectives. Thus, the healthcare consumer wants ready and easy access to health services, and less expensively too, at least in countries where the consumer pays wholly or in part for these services. The payer in publicly funded health systems, such as in Canada, wants to deliver high quality healthcare but also has concerns about escalating health spending, hence wants to curtail it, as do employers reeling under the yoke of health benefits to their workers for example, GM, and Ford. The GP wants to deliver excellent, evidence-based healthcare, but has limited financial resources to invest in the technologies required to achieve this goal. As divergent as the objectives of some healthcare stakeholders may be to the realization of these dual healthcare delivery objectives, for example, those of the private health insurer, or even of pharmaceutical companies, driven by what many would consider primarily profit motives, they converge on global considerations of the issues involved. The profit motive of some of these stakeholders indeed on the surface seems inconsistent with the dual objectives, private health insurers for example, seeking claims reduction via restrictions of health services utilization, or imposing higher premiums that exclude effectively some from access to health services ostensibly to mitigate moral hazard. There is also no doubt that pharmaceutical companies want to sell their medications, on which in most cases they have invested millions of dollars in research and development (R&D), among others. Technology firms also want to sell their high-tech products, such as CAT scanners, and MRI equipments. It is quite understandable that many would contend that such motives and the achievement of the dual healthcare delivery objectives mentioned earlier are dissimilar, even incompatible. On scrutiny however, as we would attempt to show, these stakeholders could not be striving at different goals than the dual healthcare delivery objectives without being internally inconsistent, at which juncture, it also becomes clear that the issue of doctors and their use or otherwise of computers, and of healthcare ICT, becomes pivotal to the future of health systems. By extension, it also does to those of the different healthcare stakeholders. As custodians of information, customarily, for example, doctors know the important role they play in passing this on to their patients, sharing it with their colleagues, and ensuring its safety and security, among others. Many individuals still depend on their doctors to provide the health information they need, despite the ubiquity of the Internet and other contemporary information portals. They often view the information received from their doctors as more accurate and meaningful than that obtained elsewhere, mainly because of the trust and mutual respect inherent in the age-old doctor-patient relationship. Indeed, they expect their doctors to have current information on a health matters, which many do now, although which they would likely find increasingly difficult to do considering the fast pace of information generation in the health industry, from clinical work and research findings, among others. Most patients for example should not have to subscribe to the American Journal of Epidemiology to know as in its September 2006 issue1, that an individual s body mass index (BMI) and waist circumference are satisfactory to gauge their health risks due to excess weight, at least among older men, according to a recent study by UK researchers. This is important information that their family doctors ought to be able to provide, in particular to those that most urgently need it. This is even more so considering the recent controversy over the value of BMI vis-à-vis waist-to-hip ratio(WHR)/waist circumference, with some recent studies asserting that the latter better conveys the effect of lean body mass and fat mass on health, hence is more predictive of mortality risk2, 3, in particular in individuals over 75 years. The U.K researchers also noted the close relationship between BMI, waist circumference, and fat mass index, and their link to disability, poor health, and risk factors for heart disease and diabetes for examples, high blood pressure and low levels LDL, or good cholesterol, which again, is important information patients would likely expect to hear from their GPs. They should also know that although having a low fat-free mass index correlates with a higher risk of cancer and poor respiratory function it does not alone show a relationship with other health or disability measures, according to the study. As the researchers aptly noted, It is clear in our study that measures of body fat, such as body mass index and waist circumference, are good indicators of adverse health outcomes Using these simple measures of adiposity should be encouraged to reduce the public health burden of obesity and overweight in the elderly, by the promotion of lifestyles that decrease the weight gain accompanying the aging process. Even if the healthcare consumer did not seek such information, and seniors in particular seek most of their health information from their doctors, and are increasingly suave enough to ask, and in fact would be even more likely to do so as baby boomers become elderly, should the doctor not offer it? Research studies have shown the increasing public interest in health information and many seek this information on the Internet, although concerns about unequal access to information, or a digital divide, persists4 even in countries such as the U.S., where over 110 million have access to the Internet for health information5.

Furthermore, a recent study published in the British Journal of Psychiatry6, showed that people use the Internet more than they trust it. Should doctors not make themselves key allies of their patients, therefore, in the quest by the latter for health information, considering the trust many have in them? Would the doctor in fact not also be helping the health system achieve its dual healthcare delivery objectives doing so? Some might ask what the doctor has to gain, although they probably should be asking what the doctor has to lose, or should they not? Besides the fact that they are simply doing their job in keeping with their professional obligation, because not doing harm does not necessarily mean overt and direct harm, but encompasses not committing errors of omission, in particular, deliberately, doctors are also helping keep their jobs doing so. Here again, some would ask how they could have a job with everyone healthy, the response to which is that the disease model does not have to be and would not necessarily remain the basis for medical practice. Even as talk of pre-empting disease gains currency, rooted in the potential of genomics and proteonomics, among others to enable us detect and prevent the emergence of potentially flawed, disease-bearing genes, the disease implicitly even hitherto unknown, it is still a relatively long way off before even our current disease prevention efforts would eliminate all known diseases. Assuming that we would even attain this state in the future, the reinventing of medical practice to focus on how we get there would create significant opportunities for doctors to remain employed gainfully, as they contribute immensely to our traversing the pathways to this disease-free destination.

Meantime, and as an Australian Institute of Health and Welfare published on September 01, 2006, showed, even the added years improved health services and medical care offer might have a downside, regarding health, creating challenges for health systems, particularly in countries with aging populations. This research, which looked at changes in life expectancy and quality of life between 1988 and 2003, indicated that non-indigenous Australian men gained two years longer than they did in 1988, but that women who gained one year, but continue to live longer than men, would spend only six weeks of that time disability-free7. These men born in 2003 could expect to live for 77 years, versus 82 years, for women born in the same year, but up to 20 of those years with a disability, about one third of which, particularly with much difficulty, with the disability severe. As the president of the Australian Association of Gerontologists, Professor Tony Broe noted, The prospect is that we ll be able to tackle some of the disability we re seeing. But it s not great news for those who are getting into their late old age. He also noted the not as robust success in addressing disabilities in old age as there has been in preventing and controlling many diseases throughout life. Do these findings, which we could extrapolate to other countries with an aging population, not underscore the changing dynamics of healthcare delivery drivers of which, not just doctors but also all healthcare- stakeholders should be aware? Do they also not point toward the likely influence of these drivers on the nature and distribution of doctors and the roles that they play in the healthcare delivery process in the near future, rather than that they would all become jobless? According to Professor Broe, We certainly must be getting healthier because the incidence of the fatal disease is dropping in every area - hearts, lungs, kidney - all of those are dropping, except in the non-indigenous community. But it doesn t seem to be accompanied by a compression or a reduction in disability. That might be the way we measure it, in part, but it looks as though we re living longer but with the same level of disability. Indeed, the situation might even be worse since the self-report basis of the study might reveal underestimates particularly in the over 80-85 year age groups, because the main cause of disability in individuals in the age groups being neuro degenerative brain diseases, compromising reasoning abilities or those to appreciate their problems, they tend not to participate in surveys. Furthermore, other studies have suggested that the greater number of years lived with disability or daily activity constraints by women may be due to their longer survival of women after they developed these problems8. Indeed, a study on health expectancies of older Australians revealed that between 1988 1998, 75% or more of the gain in female life expectancy was with disability, all severity levels combined, even worse for males for whom this applied to virtually all the extra years of expected life9. Should we therefore, not in fact anticipate even higher disabilities levels, in particular due to the neuro degenerative disorders of ageing, in the next decade or two as baby boomers reach their late seventies and eighties? Does this potential spike in disabilities among seniors not call for health reforms to address this and related problems? Do we not need to revisit out approaches to issues such as the availability of resources for the training of doctors and other healthcare professionals, or the development of programs at the primary, secondary, and tertiary disease prevention levels, especially the last tier, with the appropriate treatment and rehabilitation resources established to prevent/tackle disease sequelae? There is thus, likely to be an increasing variety of roles for doctors in the healthcare delivery process, as they persist in their current roles and take on the additional tasks the disabilities that we mentioned above impose as the latter increasingly assume the healthcare center-stage. The point here is that medical practice is changing paradigms in keeping with changing times, and doctors not only nee to be cognizant of these changes but also to be flexible and be ready to adapt to these changes, for example to appreciate the increasingly significant roles that healthcare ICT plays in the many processes that result in healthcare delivery. However, before we dwell on the burgeoning relationships between doctors and these technologies, let us mention some developments in the health sector that would inevitably even heighten these relationships. Perhaps the most pertinent is the re-emergence of the concept of population health, with increasing emphasis on the three-tiered disease prevention approach mentioned above, health promotion, both physical and mental, and on health and wellness rather than on disease. This explains the point we made earlier about the changing model of medical or health practice, and does the increasing varieties of practice models we see in contemporary healthcare such as payers offering doctors incentives to incorporate disease prevention and health promotion in their practices in some countries. There is also a proliferation of health and wellness centres, some as standalone enterprises, others parts of existing practices. With the increasing patient-centredness of healthcare delivery would be even more attempts by healthcare providers to differentiate their practices by offering enhanced value propositions to their clients, whose preferences for health services are already in fact increasingly suave, the emphasis likely to be on total health packages across the lifespan, for this ever-more discerning clientele. There would also be providers seeking such differentiation raising entry barriers to their practices by their competitors via the use of sophisticated technologies, including healthcare ICT, or offering niche services, for example cardiac, orthopaedic, cancer treatment, among others. In fact, there has been resurgence in recent times in physician-owned niche hospitals in countries such as the United States, the advance of

which hospitals, aborted around 2003 as federal regulators slammed a provisional funding ban, seems this time unstoppable as federal funding becomes available again, and new developments in health are rife, however, so are concerns for some. Among the concerns are that these hospitals could deplete an already overstrained health care system of its well-off clientele, the poorest and most-ill remaining, and that profit motive could compromise service delivery by their doctor-owners. The hospitals supporters, and there are over 200 of such hospitals now in the U.S., extol their efficiency, and their contributions to streamlining of medical care. As for example Dr. Blake Curd, an orthopaedic surgeon and a 2% stake-owner of the Sioux Falls Surgical Centre in South Dakota noted, We are focused factories Here I can do 10 to 12 operations by 2 or 3 in the afternoon In a general hospital, it would take two to three days to do the same. Incidentally, many would contend that doctors put their funds in these practices partly to make up for waning recompenses from Medicare, the federal health seniors insurer, and from private health plans. Concerns about niche hospitals in the U.S. depleting resources, including professional expertise from other less-financially endowed health organizations, echo similar concerns of some in Canada opposed to the establishment in the country of a parallel private health system. Recent developments in Canada, for example, the 2005 Supreme Court ruling giving Quebecois permission to proceed to seek private healthcare, have given impetus to the call in other provinces and territories for a parallel private health system, and although it is unclear whether this would happen on a large scale or if at all, it would, the debate continues. Regardless of the debate s outcome though, the issues regarding changing doctors role in the healthcare delivery process would remain, as even if they remained in the publicly funded health system, the exigencies of the interplay of the variety of drivers of healthcare delivery would mandate a review of the status of doctors in the healthcare delivery process. This review would in fact start with the doctors themselves as they attempt to fulfill the obligations of their changing roles in keeping with their sworn oath to deliver the best healthcare to their patients, although would likely also involve inter-sectoral collaboration as doctors interface with other professionals and domains in the course of their duties. In other words, doctors would be hard -pressed to remain oblivious for too long, if at all, for example, to the needs of the health system to achieve to achieve the dual healthcare delivery objectives, as this would run counter to their interests also, professional, ethical, even financial, among others, even if in the long term. Similarly, they would have to embrace certain developments and trends occurring in both the health and non-health domains of healthcare delivery, in other that they do not compromise the progress toward the increased efficiency and cost-effectiveness that the variety of changes taking place in the health sector overall aims to achieve.

In this regard, it is hardly surprising that the US Centres for Medicare and Medicaid Services concluded earlier in August 2006 that doctors operating niche hospitals were not grossing disproportionate ROI, although it added new financial disclosure rules, with a $10,000 a day fine for example, if they did not file on time reports on financial reimbursement for their doctors. It also obliged the hospitals to treat emergency patients. Besides the fact of their revenues, which some dispute, arguing that these doctors in fact make recommendations that disproportionately increase these revenues, although their conclusions that this creates a medical arms race that soars health costs is arguable, these hospitals do not force anyone to patronize them. In fact, that the healthcare consumer has the prerogative to choose his/ her provider is at the core of the new consumer-centric healthcare delivery model that is gaining increasing currency worldwide. This is the crux of the matter regarding doctors and the new imperative to embrace the means to perform their jobs more efficiently and cost-effectively, including the use of healthcare ICT, and indeed, for their practices to survive, let alone thrive in the new healthcare delivery dispensation, and this has nothing to do with a health system s funding model. If we started from the premise that the healthcare consumer could choose which doctor to see, we ought to make it possible for him/her to make rational choices. It is harder if at all possible to make such choices without the relevant information, such as the pricing of services, the expertise of the professionals in the practice, the quality of services the practice provides, such as medical error rates, mortality rates for certain surgical procedures, and readmission rates for certain illnesses, and so forth. The healthcare consumer also needs to have information on medications costs, costs of hospitalizations, and the hospitality services available and their costs, among others. Would family doctors able to provide their clients with as much information as possible about a niche hospital to which an imminent referral heads not have competitive advantage over others that would or could not do so? Would this not mean for those that want to offer such information to have the means to obtain it, and does this not underscore the need for implementing not just the relevant healthcare ICT, but to be able to access the required information through collaboration with those niche hospitals, via an integrated information network for example? Would these developments not in fact reduce healthcare costs for the consumer as more family doctors and niche hospitals compete on value-added propositions for healthcare consumer patronage? Could this already be happening and was why CMS reached its conclusions about the returns on investments by these hospitals not being disproportionate? In relation to the roughly 5,000 general hospitals in the U.S, the doctor-owned group is minuscule, although major chains such as Universal Health Services Inc. and Triad Hospitals Inc. have raised alarms that the niche hospitals are reducing their profits in key markets. Would this not in fact inspire the necessary changes in these chains to enable them com pete more effectively in a changing healthcare delivery milieu? Would they therefore not eventually as some are in fact already doing, put pressure on healthcare providers to embrace the technologies that could enhance their competitiveness? Would embracing g these technologies not ultimately be a survival imperative for these providers? With the rapid proliferation of these niche hospitals, Texas alone having fifty eight doctor-owned hospitals, and over twenty others awaiting approval as the ban lapses, and similar developments occurring right across the country, this competition could only escalate, with benefits down the road for not just the healthcare consumer, but also the providers, payers, and the health system at large. Even if physicians self-refer to their niche hospitals, the patient is not bound to go there. If they did, based on their preferences it is within their rights to do so. It is therefore moot to argue that these doctors have a conflict of interest. In fact, it is counter-intuitive for them to refer patients to other doctors when they have the expertise and resources to treat the patient just as effectively. The caveat is that the patient has to have all the facts to agree with the referral, which underscores the need for them also to have information on other comparable health providers and facilities to make rational choices. This again points to the need for more comprehensive information portals for this purpose, which hospitals, state or provincial health information web sites, even private entrepreneurs could provide via dedicated web-based services for example, free or even for a small fee. Besides its yearly database of Health Plan Employer Data and Information Set (HEDIS(r)) and Accreditation information from the country s health plans, a free, online version of the U.S. National Committee for Quality Assurance s (NCQA) Quality Dividend Calculator (QDC) is now available at www.ncqacalculator.com. The database has performance data and member satisfaction information of hundreds of health plans, and the calculator enables employers and other users to know how well health plans in their locale manage illnesses, which provide the best value, and how their services impact absenteeism and productivity, actually making it possible to predict sick offs, and potential savings from lost productivity. As we noted earlier, the changes occurring in both health and non -health domains relevant to healthcare delivery are simply too formidable for doctors to ignore. Is it possible for example to discountenance the results of the Australian Institute of Health and Welfare mentioned earlier regarding the likely increase in disabilities among seniors in the coming years. These disabilities are in fact not all going to be neurocognitive, although these might be the causes of others for example fractures due to falls that such neurocognitive disabilities directly or indirectly occasion. Could they ignore the variety of assistive technologies with which they could monitor their elderly patients at home, including those that help prevent such falls or alert someone to them, that are streaming into the markets lately? There is no doubt that such consumer demand would increasingly play a major role in the nature and extent of patronage healthcare providers receive, for example which niche hospitals would, with almost 77 million baby boomers nearing the age many would require hip and knee replacement for examples, or even new hearts. Furthermore, with regard niche hospitals, Medicare and private insurers, reimburse their services, say orthopaedic treatment, better than for say, the flu, or even some chronic illnesses. Is there a lesson for doctors thus that in the fact, specialty hospitals essentially aim to treat healthier patients? Could this be a key driver of the sort of eclectic choice of practice models we would increasingly see in healthcare delivery in the future, and does this create even more opportunities for doctors rather than stifle them? The point here is that not all doctors should have to compete in the niche specialty market. As we have seen, these markets match certain doctors and certain patients, best. Doctors would have to decide in which market they wish to operate based on their expertise first, and on their value propositions and of course other key individual considerations. In other words, doctors would increasingly need to be creative in offering health services that people need. They would need to start remodelling their mindset, thinking outside the box literally, and coming up with marketable health services. They would have to essentially be more marketing-oriented, understand the health needs of the populace they serve, and offer them the needed services. Doctors would also have to be flexible enough to adapt their choice of practice model as necessary, in particular regarding the deployment of appropriate healthcare ICT to acquire competitive edge, for example, implementing customer relationship management (CRM) software to boost the practice s front-end operations in today s healthcare environment where distinctive customer care could significantly increase market share. The challenge of the niche hospitals continues to trigger a variety of responses from major hospital chains for example, some such as Triad, offering doctors equity stakes, and the American Federation of Hospitals trade group aiming for more restrictions on the niche hospitals. The real issue though, as we noted earlier, is to opt for competition or not with these niche hospitals. The former choice would require attempting to provide better services than the niche hospitals on whatever benchmarks the competitor decides, for examples service quality and/or pricing. Doctors in niche hospitals place high premiums on the quality of their services, and often argue that their expertise results in better treatment outcomes, although a recent Medicare study noted mixed results on quality for these hospitals, that they tend to have lower adverse events but also higher re-admission rates. The study noted further that because they treat healthier patients, comparisons might be slanted, which underscores the point about the suitability of the market for particular providers, but also that of the existence of other potential markets, for example, for the management of the chronically ill, in which doctors could compete more favourably with their peers. The fact remains though, that they would still need to compete, with all its implications for service differentiation, and the use of appropriate healthcare information and communications technologies for example, to achieve this objective. As we also noted earlier, the need for such differentiation is crucial to contemporary healthcare delivery and would be even more so in the near future for a variety of reasons. It also has nothing to do with whether the doctor practices in a publicly- or privately-funded health system. In the first place, the goals of healthcare delivery remain the same regardless of a health system s funding model. In other words, any health system that does not deliver qualitative health services efficiently and cost-effectively would eventually collapse.

Apart from the fact that resources are limited, financial, and otherwise, health systems cannot continue to expend increasing amounts of their gross domestic product (GDP) to fund health services. Indeed, that itself, suggests there is something wrong with the health system, as in fact they should spend less as the overall health of the populace improves. Indeed, research has shown that increased health spending does not necessarily translate into improved overall healthcare10. Some argue with regard to Canada, for example that the country could afford to spend 11.5% of its GDP on health for the next 25 years population aging and an extra $7 billion per year increase in health spending, regardless11. The projections, based on the assumptions that the quality of health care remains the same, at its 2000-01 level and that there are no future extra spending pressures, could clearly not hold. It is inconceivable that the quality of care a health system expects to provide would remain static even for a moment not to mention for 25 years, and it is inconsistent with what some would consider the frenetic pace of medical knowledge generation to expect changes with the potential to strain the system, not to occur for so long. The unexpected emergence in recent years, of novel viral diseases, for examples, SARS, and avian flu is instructive in this regard. Besides, it is only prudent to attempt to curtail seemingly runaway health spend ing when alternative approaches exist that could ensure the achievement of the dual health delivery objectives mentioned earlier. Indeed, rather than encourage investments in expensive high-tech, such as MRI and CT scanners, which some blame for the increasing health spending, and curtailing expenditure on which some consider advocates of fiscal restraints attempts to compromise the quality of healthcare delivery, these approaches promote rational resource allocation on these costly technologies, and their appropriate utilization. Thus, the issue is not that health systems should not invest in these technologies, but that they should do so in a rational manner their implementation as economically feasible as their clinical justification for so doing, rational. It would therefore be unnecessary for example to have a CT scanner in every hospital in the country, much as it would not, to have a hospital in every town. Does it make any economic sense to have one in a hospital that is only minimally used, say five times in a year for example, when another town just five minutes away also has one, and with a much higher utilization rate? Would it not be more rational, economically to have those five patients taken by ambulance to the nearby town to have their CT scans done? Would it not also be more clinically rational to have the ambulance equipped with wireless information systems that could relay patient monitoring data in-transit to the ER of the hospitals and with which paramedics could receive crucial information and directives on patient handling and treatment en-route the hospital? Would this ambulance not serve useful purposes for other patients as well? Would this not be a more prudent way to utilize resources than invest on an idle CT scanner, which would also incur running and maintenance costs? This example clearly illustrates the point about the so-called, fiscal approaches to healthcare delivery, that it is not an attempt to compromise but rather to improve healthcare delivery quality, at the same time reducing health spending. It also exemplifies the changing dynamics of healthcare drivers that doctors need to imbibe mentioned earlier, regardless of the funding model of the health system in which they practice. Would it not be useful in patient management for example, for the family doctor of the patient to be in the information loop, receiving and communicating crucial patient information with the paramedics, and the host hospital s ER doctor that could contribute to more effective care delivery if not even save the patient s life? Would this not require the family doctor to embrace and implement healthcare ICT, and would the doctor and his/her practice not benefit in reputation and by extension patronage providing such high quality care that would differentiate the practice from its competitors, and provide perhaps, much-needed competitive advantage in the locale? A new study involving the use by SUNY Upstate Medical University physicians of traffic surveillance cameras to view motor vehicle crashes and rescue operations on Central New York highways, further highlights the potential benefits of such integrated networks of disparate information systems in improving healthcare delivery12. By enabling the real-time view of crash scenes, the system offers ER doctors information that could improve care provision to crash victims when they arrive at the ER, the potential for life saving further enhanced the system integrated with the ambulance health information systems mentioned earlier. The study, U.S. economist Alfred Kahn, who survived a 2003 car crash and was for weeks, hospitalized in SUNY Upstate s teaching hospital, University Hospital, is funding, will give the researchers access to almost 20 closed -circuit video cameras installed in and around Syracuse by the NY state Department of Transportation (DOT), and monitored by the DOT's Syracuse office round the clock. A special receiving antenna delivers real time images into a customized workstation (by CXtec) near the hospital s trauma room, where doctors and other healthcare professionals could view the crash scene and rescue activities. DOT staff would alert the researchers to a crash and notify them of the camera on which to view it, the latter then able to record the images and instruct the DOT staff on camera zooming/panning for the best view. According to John McCabe, M.D., professor and chair of the Department of Emergency Medicine at SUNY Upstate, We think the ability to view real time images of the accident scene to see the extent of damage and the response from paramedics can provide us with a wealth of information that may help us better treat the accident victims when they arrive at the emergency room. Now, first responders (paramedics) to a crash scene communicate with doctors by radio regarding the accident scene based on eyewitness accounts if possible, and the nature and extent of injuries of affected persons. Noting McCabe, The information we get from the scene is what we relay on to mobilize staff and equipment in the emergency room before the patient arrives and often this information can be ambiguous. To illustrate the potential confusion, of course with cost implications that such imprecise information could engender, a couple of years ago, initial reports on an early morning crash involving three cars that occurred on Interstate 90 near Syracuse, indicated the involvement of twenty three persons. The University Hospital s ER staff instantaneously sprung into action in readiness to receive the patients including initiating efforts to move ER patients to other units, and calling up additional ER staff, only a while later to realize that just six patients were on their way to the hospital. As McCabe again aptly observes, This is a good example of how being able to see the scene in real time and being able to communicate more closely with the emergency personnel at the scene, would have allowed our staff to better anticipate the patient needs By viewing the scene, we would have been able to see early on that many of these individuals were walking wounded and were not going to be coming to the hospital. Indeed, studies carried out in the U.S. such as those done at East Carolina University and Albany Medical College, have indicated that doctors have benefited regarding patient management from being able to view images of crash scenes, including the damage to vehicles12. The ECU and AMC studies also showed that ER doctors that viewed the images noted the accidents were more severe than the reports paramedics gave. Would a public health system with the technology backbone for such seamless integration of intersectoral systems with the health information systems of the ER, other doctors and healthcare professionals, including the family doctor, and with those of the health jurisdiction in which they operate not be creating the enabling milieu for the competitiveness it needs to remain viable? Would this not help it, say a public-funded health system, prevent the depletion of its patient base by, and let us assume a technologically-loaded private health organization? Should doctors not be working in tandem with other healthcare professionals and indeed, relevant other non-health sectors in facilitating the realization of the deployment of the healthcare ICT on which the future of healthcare delivery in the man, rests? Furthermore, public health systems are accountable for the management of their budgets, and must do so responsibly, even without the need to ward off competition from a parallel private health system. They also need to deliver high quality health services within these budgetary constraints, which they would easier do, were they to create such enabling technology infrastructure to which family doctors, and other healthcare professionals could connect their health information systems, an integration that would facilitate patient information communication and sharing and improve the quality of healthcare delivery. The corollary is also true, as without such infrastructure, or its integration with the health information systems of these healthcare providers, patients could not expect to access let alone receive the best quality care. This means a progressive increase in morbidity and mortality, which would further increase the costs of care and the country s overall health spending, a situation that would reverberate throughout the entire economy compromising the finances of every healthcare stakeholder one way or another. This underscores the point we made earlier about the unlikelihood of doctors, or any healthcare stakeholder for that matter deliberately jeopardizing the health system. Nonetheless, that doctors are slow to adopt healthcare ICT, which studies, including one by the Rand Corp. that showed that national adoption of the EHRs in the U.S could result in over $81 billion in annual savings, and others that have shown could help health systems achieve the dual healthcare delivery objectives mentioned earlier remains troubling13.

To be sure, one should not dismiss the fact that doctors have reasons for shunning these technologies, whose rates of adoption also varies with countries. That some doctors are technophobes is not in doubt, nor is the hindrance to healthcare ICT acquisition attributable to the costs of these technologies. Some studies have even questioned the ability of the technologies to improve healthcare delivery and save costs if they, specifically electronic health records (EHR) result in increased billing, compromised the productivity of doctors, and had to effect on provider-to-patient ratios14. In particular, the author argued that hospitals would pass on the installation and maintenance costs of EHRs to the consumer via increased billings, and that costs would increase rapidly if these technologies did not improve the quality and efficiency of healthcare delivery. Beside the point that they would, particularly if not only more doctors and other healthcare professionals embrace them, but also implement many of the advanced features of say EMR systems expected to highlight the improvements in care delivery and reduce costs, and even if EHR implementations could result in short-term physician productivity decline, the long-term benefits outweigh the short-term handicaps. Furthermore, the findings underscore the need for improvements in these technologies that would result in shorter learning curves, which might partly explain the productivity issues, in addition to incomplete installation of the technologies features mentioned earlier. Incidentally, the author noted the potential value of EHRs to facilitate pay-for-performance (P4P) programs and in managing the chronically ill. These are both key issues in the direction healthcare services head in many countries hence of the need to be mindful of the key role healthcare ICT could play in this process. In many developed and even some developing countries, the demographic shift toward an increasingly aging population is going to make the management, including the prevention and treatment of chronic diseases even more pressing a major health issue in the coming years, for example. Considering the benefits to the management of these diseases that even this study that does not seem that favourably to healthcare ICT noted should doctors not increasingly adopt these technologies, particularly those practicing in countries whose population is rapidly aging? How could such a doctor hope to practice effectively and efficiently and to contribute to the realization of the dual healthcare delivery objectives, positively, otherwise? In countries such as the U.S, and consequent to the increasing public concern of healthcare delivery quality, private and public third-party payers are toying with pecuniary inducements, P4P, that recompense doctors for suggested (evidence-based) care, which implies the need for doctors to be aware of such recommended treatment approaches. This again underlines the need for doctors to implement the necessary communication, data, document, knowledge, or model-driven decision support systems (DSS) to be aware of and receive regular updates on changes to such recommended care and related patient management issues, although some criticize the practice s implementation complexity, but also the tradeoffs marred by ambiguity involved in determining who receives what. Others argue that P4P incentives might improve care quality for some patients, but reduce it or access to care for other patients, and that they could promote improper care or restrict care access for poor patients or those with multiple disorders. Here again, we see the significance of healthcare ICT deployment in resolving these issues, and the role doctors could play in helping to achieve this objective, embracing the technologies that could do so. These technologies would not only ensure that doctors follow the recommendations for the management of particular disorders, they could help determine the roles each doctor plays in the management process, and in the determination of the recompense each receives based on the expected outcomes for example of each intervention vis-à-vis the final management outcome. This would be relevant in particular with regard patients with chronic and multiple illnesses, most of who would be the elderly, whose population would increase significantly in many developed countries over the coming years hence the need to pay serious attention to these issues and for doctors to contribute to their solutions by adopting healthcare ICT. Indeed, Medicare, the U.S. federal health care scheme for seniors and disabled, has started using provider-focused P4P incentives. Some consider that Congress could achieve the potential of provider focused P4P inducements simultaneously lessening the downside to the program confining it to private Medicare Advantage plans and by promoting increased participation in the plans, as well as targeting the inducements at doctors and patients alike, these suggestions, indicative of the significance of P4P to future healthcare delivery. In fact, a recent issue by Alliance for Health Reform indicated that CMS s P4P is showing impressive results in improving the quality of healthcare delivery and cutting down healthcare costs, particular, out of its, over 100 P4P now in progress, its Premier Hospital Quality Incentive Demonstration. This recompenses the top 20% of hospitals with notable scores on 33 indicators for five disorders. It also cuts Medicare compensation for hospitals that fall short of defined thresholds. The project, in its first nine months showed an average improvement for the 260 participating hospitals of 6.6%, most gains made in community-acquired pneumonia and heart failure. No doubt, with an increase in P4P s acceptance would the debate over the amount and structure of its inducements rise, as would on issues regarding the sanctions needed to trigger quality w hist not reproving providers treating the most ill, and others for example setting up preventive measures for services under/over-utilization as providers jostle for inducements. Involving patients in the incentives program also underscores the point about the need for more widespread diffusion of healthcare information and communications technologies, not just among doctors but actually all healthcare stakeholders. Such bi-directional incentive programs have the potential to improve further the quality of healthcare delivery since patients could liaise with their doctors better in determining appropriate management eliminating the potential for abuse of the system and resource wastage, thereby saving costs, while still ensuring the delivery of qualitative healthcare. However, would such liaison not be m ore effective and efficient both doctors and patients able to communicate via integrated healthcare ICT networks, for example, patients implementing personal health records (PHR) integrated with their doctors EMR? How could doctors expect to persuade their patients to implement such technologies when they themselves lack the EMR technologies to which they would connect? Would such doctors in fact not be compromising their practices patients, who have PHR, as many of the suave baby boomers that would become future seniors probably would, requesting such hook ups only to discover the doctors did not have EMR? This again, highlights the point we made earlier that the changes that would probably be taking place in various domains of the healthcare delivery enterprise would likely leave doctors keen for their practices to survive if not thrive in the near future little choice but to literally join the healthcare ICT bandwagon. This, among other reasons is why doctors need to start to make the necessary adjustments to their healthcare delivery worldview even now. Granted that other healthcare stakeholders should encourage doctors to adopt these technologies, which is already the case with governments, for example that of Alberta offering its doctors money to implement them, as with others for examples software vendors, health insurance firms, and even major employers, doctors should realize that it is in their best interests to do so. As we noted earlier, it is also in the interests of their countries that doctors d o so. With health spending continuing to increase in many countries, among Organization for Economic Co-operation and Development (OECD) countries, for example mainly due to expensive medical technologies, hospitalizations, prescription medications, and aging populations, pressure is on in many of these countries to curtail these soaring healthcare costs15. Health spending made up almost 9% of GDP on average across OECD countries in 2004, versus 7% in 1990, the public sector paying for much of these costs in these countries beside the U.S. and Mexico, 73% of health spending publicly funded on the average (Chart 1.)

Chart 1. Change in health expenditure as a share of GDP, OECD countries, 1990 and 2004

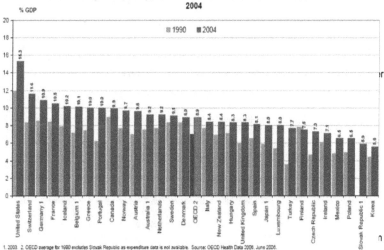

1. 2003 2. OECD average for 1990 excludes Slovak Republic as expenditure data is not available. Source: OECD Health Data 2006, June 2006.

Out-of-pocket health spending that is direct private payments for health, and private health insurance payments are notable sources of health funding in these countries, too, 51% in Mexico, the highest and in Australia, out-of-pocket spending, 22% of total health spending in 2002/03 (Chart 2.) The OECD Health Data 200615 also showed that health spending has increased faster than GDP in all OECD cou ntries other than Finland from 1990 to 2004, accounting for 7% of GDP on average in 1990 and 8.9% in 2004, 8.8% the previous year, health spending projected to increase even further in the years ahead (Chart 3.) These figures underscore the need for OECD countries to ensure sustainable health systems financing, , as it is inconceivable that they would continue to increase taxes, the source of the bulk of healthcare funding in these countries as noted earlier, to keep their health systems running even as healthcare costs soar.That the public percentage of health sp ending has reduced in some countries for examples, Hungary, the Czech Republic, and Poland, where it was high in 1990, and gone up in countries such as the U.S., Mexico, Switzerland and Korea, where the reverse was true, attests to the chances of this percentage going either way. In other words, it speaks to the possibility of countries curtailing their health spending, while still providing their peoples with high quality health services, the achievement of which dual healthcare delivery goals, the widespread implementation, and utilization of healthcare ICT could facilitate. Even in countries such as the U.S. where the private sector continues to be preeminent in health system financing, public spending on health per capita is still more than in most other OECD countries, due to the overall health spending in the U.S., being significantly higher than in other nations. The U.S therefore also needs to work towards achieving the dual healthcare delivery objectives, which underscores the point we made earlier that the quest to do so should not depend on the funding model of health systems.

On the other hand, it should predicate on the realization of the potential for achieving these dual goals, implementing healthcare information and communication technologies on a large scale within the health system. Why would any fiscally responsible health system want to spend money it needs not spend to achieve its goals, whatever they are, anyway? The point in fact is that even if it did, probably it could not afford and would likely become increasingly unable so to do, with the rate at which health spending is increasing in many countries, particularly in the developed world. These among other reasons make it important for doctors to consider what they could do to assist in the realization of these dual healthcare delivery goals, including the deployment of healthcare ICT in their practices.

Private health insurance is only about 6% of total health spending on average in OECD countries. However, it plays a significant part in health spending for some population groups in Germany and the Netherlands, and for the majority of the non-senior population in the U.S., 24% of health spending in 2004, in the latter country, between 10% and 15% in Canada and France, where private health insurance provide optional, enhanced coverage, to the public health systems. With private health insurance helping to pay for medications than for hospital or ambulatory care as drugs coverage in many publicly financed insurance schemes is often inadequate, the need for rational drug prescribing is only reasonable, and in any case, would become inevitable the more patients realize their chances of influencing the drugs doctors prescribe for them. Mexico had the least public coverage of spending on medications among OECD countries in 2004 at 12%, the U.S., 24%, Poland, 37%, and Canada, 38%, over 75% medications of expenditures publicly financed in countries such as Austria, France, Germany, Spain and Sweden in the same year. In many countries, health spending on medications by both private and public payers is increasing at alarming rates. The point then is that both public and private spending on medications are significant health expenditures that payers would want to curtail, and which goal, doctors, by embracing healthcare ICT could help them achieve. There are certainly a variety of software and healthcare ICT for example, the

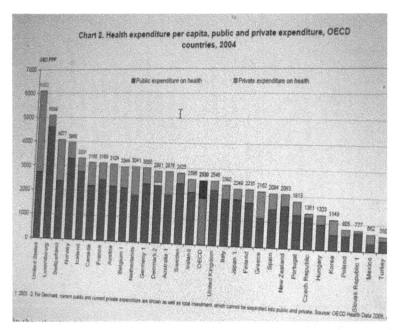

Chart 2. Health expenditure per capita, public and private expenditure, OECD countries, 2004

computerized physician order entry (CPOE) systems, which could not only help rationalize prescribing patterns, but also help reduce medical error rates, and improve patient safety, which indirectly reduces morbidity and mortality, obviating the need for additional medications use, or even hospitalizations. The more widespread use of these technologies, and indeed, other healthcare information and communication technologies, such as e-prescribing, and electronic medical records (EMR) would no doubt help in achieving the dual healthcare delivery goals. Incidentally, there is evidence of a shift in doctors attitude along this direction, as a new report in August 2006, by the U.S Centers for Disease Control and Prevention's National Center for Health Statistics, Electronic Medical Record use by Office-based Physicians: United States, 2005, showed 16.

According to this report, 23.9% of physicians, almost a quarter, reported utilizing full or partial electronic medical records (EMRs) in their office-based practice in 2005. This is an increase of 31% compared to 18.2%, in 2001. Midwest (26.9%) and West (33.4%)-based doctors were more likely to use these technologies than those based in the Northeast (14.4 %,) and those in metropolitan statistical areas (almost 24.8%) more likely than those in non-metropolitan areas (16.9%). The reported also noted, however, that just 9.3% or a tenth of total U.S. physicians, used EMRs with all four of the basic functions. These functions are computerized orders for prescriptions, computerized orders for tests, reporting of test results, and physician notes, the use of all of which is necessary not just for a total EMR system, but for the

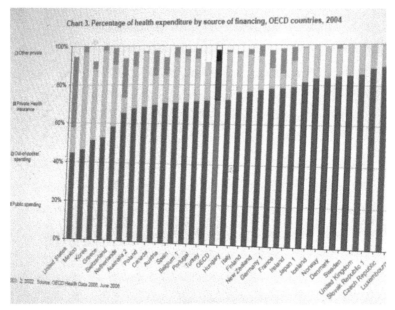

Chart 3. Percentage of health expenditure by source of financing, OECD countries, 2004

realization of the system s full potential. There might be cost issues involved in doctors not implementing these systems in full, which is why software and healthcare ICT vendors also have a part to play in promoting the widespread adoption and utilization of the technologies by doctors offering less costly EMR systems to them. These firms could also offer payment options for incremental or even full implementation, and generous licensing contracts, among other incentives, efforts from which they would reap ample rewards anyhow, as more doctors implement their systems. Additionally, over time, software and healthcare ICT would have little choice but to reduce the prices of their products and services as they become ubiquitous in the markets and increasingly more doctors implement the technologies. In other words, doctors need to realize the benefits derivable to them and their colleagues as many more of them implement these technologies, hence should keep doing so to attain the critical mass after which prices of EMR and other healthcare ICT would have to start falling, including those of licenses, and even maintenance. Thus, even the early adapters would still have a chance to save some money, not to mention the benefits, likely enduring, which their earlier adoption of these technologies would have conferred on them, in particular with regard cornering market share. As noted earlier, software firms would also generate more revenue from the expanding markets even with prices falling, and those more enterprising among them would likely generate even more carrying out comprehensive process cycle analyses on relevant market issues, hence identifying the needs of their markets of interest, and developing innovative products and services to meet these needs. The emergence on the healthcare markets of a variety of products and services to improve healthcare delivery, and by extension reduce healthcare costs would bode well for the realization of the dual healthcare delivery objectives, and doctors by embracing these technologies would have been active participants in the process. recent Harvard University/University of Michigan study buttresses the significance of investing in health. The study showed that in spite of the increases in health spending since 1960, the return on medical spending is high17. The researchers examined health expenditures between 1960 and 2000 in the U.S., and found that healthcare in America has been cost-effective overall, although expressed concerns about the soaring healthcare costs for seniors. In their New England Journal of Medicine August 31, 2006 article, the researchers we compared gains in life expectancy with the increased costs of care from 1960 through 2000, specifically, the average per-capita spending and life expectancy of four different age groups during that period, analyzing increases in medical expenses vis-à-vis improvements in health. To control for the influence of non-medical factors for examples, reduced smoking prevalence and death rates from accidents, suicide, and homicide, on survival, the researchers assumed that medical care caused half of the gains. The researchers found an increase by 6.97 years in life expectancy 69.90 to 76.87 years, for newborns during the period, and about $69,000 lifetime inflation-adjusted, medical spending increase, with the cost per year of life gained an estimated $19,900. They attributed 70% of part of the gain due to improvements in healthcare to reductions in deaths from cardiovascular disease and 19% to reductions in infant mortality. The researchers concluded that the increases in medical spending since 1960 have provided reasonable value, on average, although that for medical care for the elderly since 1980 correlated with a high cost per year of life gained , those 65 years and older having lived just 3.5 years longer since 1960, at a cost of $84,700 for each year. Commenting on the findings, one of the researchers, David M. Cutler, the Otto Eckstein Professor of Applied Economics in Harvard s Faculty of Arts and Sciences, asserted that the significant increase in life expectancy seen in the country over the years amply justified its rising medical costs. Does this study not in fact also support our assertion thus far that it would even be more rational to deliver qualitative health services simultaneously reducing health spending? As Cutler noted, The foremost cause of concern posed by rising medical costs is the tremendous strain coming from increased costs for the elderly The cost per year of life for seniors is three times higher today than it was in the 1970s. Does this observation not support further the need for health systems to aim to achieve the dual healthcare delivery objectives, in particular in countries with an aging population? Indeed, the researchers also noted that rising costs could lead to diminishing returns as life expectancy plateaus, and that the significant improvement in the quality of life for the elderly supports the current levels of healthcare spending among the elderly, but how sustainable is this or rational is it considering the diminishing returns mentioned earlier? In other words, should we not be seeking ways to sustain this improvement in the quality of life for seniors without incurring seemingly ever-increasing costs? With the options available so to do, for example investing more in and promoting the widespread implementation and utilization of healthcare information and communication technologies, should our efforts not focus in this direction? Do doctors not have a major role to play in this regard? These findings also point to the need for doctors, mentioned earlier to appreciate the importance of being flexible in their approaches to medical practice to be able to recognize opportunities for novel value propositions to their patients and adjust their practice accordingly to deliver these services and products as the case may be to them. In other words, again as we noted earlier, other models of care would likely emerge in the years ahead driven by advances in medical knowledge and progress in technology, including in healthcare software and other ICT. Indeed, the future landscape of healthcare delivery would be an amalgam of health and non-health enterprises engaged in a continuous exercise of exploration of the intercalating issues that result in healthcare delivery. These explorations would essentially be enduring decomposition/exposition cycles that would result in more in-depth appreciation of theses issues and how their interplay pans out in the determination of the outcome, namely, healthcare delivery, but also could reveal even cryptic issues with the potential for novel value propositions. These propositions would be multidirectional, with software and other healthcare ICT firms for example presenting innovative products and services to meet identified healthcare needs, patients expectations of care inspiring such value propositions by doctors, and software vendors, and doctors new knowledge base, triggering the need for new software to deliver certain services or to improve the delivery of others. Thus, we see the likely emergence of a new era in healthcare delivery of which doctors could hardly afford not to be a part. Indeed, they would likely be key players in the evolution of the seismic changes that healthcare delivery would undergo in the years ahead, although this would likely be in concert with other key players, including the patients themselves. For this and other reasons, it is in all doctors best interests to embrace and adopt the technologies that would be pivotal to these imminent changes, namely healthcare information and communication technologies. A recent study by economists Kenneth Thorpe and David Howard published in Health Affairs online on August 22, 200618 showed that almost all the increase in U.S., Medicare spending over the past 15 years is attributable to patients treated for five or more medical conditions during the year. The authors thought this was due to both an increase in factual disease prevalence and modifications in clinical treatment thresholds. According to the study, these beneficiaries alone made up 76% of total Medicare spending in 2002, versus 52.2% in 1987. Noted, Thorpe and Howard of Emory University s Rollins School of Public Health, regarding the role of obesity in increasing health spending, which is substantially higher, increases in the share of non-obese beneficiaries treated for five or more medical conditions show that there are other factors at work . Importantly also, the authors queried the fit of how Medicare reimburses services for complex medical management based on their findings that for the metabolic syndrome, which they utilized as a case study, the share of patients treated with medications went up 11.5% points in less than a decade. Besides highlighting, the problems associated with reimbursements, which as we noted earlier with P4P, are critical issues in the future of healthcare delivery, these findings also underscore the need for rational patient management, which also we discussed earlier. Again, for both issues, we should stress the important roles that healthcare ICT would play in teasing out the contributions to diagnosis and treatment, hence the health benefits of our investments and the appropriateness of our reimbursements mechanisms, and in the widespread adoption of evidence-based practice, for examples. These issues further underline the place of doctors in the overall healthcare delivery scheme, hence the significance of their playing their roles effectively as these bear crucially on the success or otherwise of the healthcare delivery efforts into which many other healthcare stakeholders input. The increasing adoption of healthcare ICT by doctors in indeed, inevitable. These technologies would constitute integral parts of medical practice of the future for the reasons we have discussed so far and many others. Healthcare delivery is moving fast in this direction but there are still obstacles in the way. Examples of such issues are concerns about the privacy and security of patient health information, the issues of the establishment of and agreement on technical standards, interoperability of disparate health information systems, the costs of healthcare software and other healthcare ICT, and issues regarding end -user buy-in, among others. Work is ongoing to solve these problems, and remove the hindrance to progress they create. In the U.S. for example, an increasing number of regional health information organizations (RHIOs) and health information exchanges (HIEs), such as Boston and Indianapolis RHIOs, and Mendocino Health Records Exchange, Boston and Indianapolis RHIOs have been implementing Connecting For Health s Common Framework. This Framework offers technology and policy resources for private and secure health-information exchange deployment its recommendations many experts deem even surpass state privacy laws and even the HIPAA provisions. However, being still in prototype since mid -2005, essentially work-in-progress, it has privacy holes , for example the PHR not authenticated by a physician. Nonetheless, efforts in solving this and other issues continue apace, and would in time yield desired results.

References

1. Available at:

http://today.reuters.co.uk/news/articlenews.aspx?type=healthNews&storyID=200
6-08-30T164639Z_01_KNE060350_RTRIDST_0_HEALTH-BMI-OBESITY- HEALTH-DC.XML Accessed on
September 01, 2006

2. Am J Clin Nutr. 2006; 118:669-682.

Available at: http://www.medscape.com/viewarticle/542661 Accessed on September 01, 2006

3. Lofgren. I, Herron. K, Zern. T, West. K, Patalay. M, Shachter. N, Koo. S and Maria Luz Fernandez. Waist
Circumference Is a Better Predictor than Body Mass Index of Coronary Heart Disease Risk in Overweight
Premenopausal Women
J. Nutr. 134:1071-1076, May 2004

4. Lorenz. D and Park. H. Web-based consumer health information: public access, digital division, and
remainders. : MedGenMed. 2006 Apr 4; 8(2):4.

5. Smith PK, Fox AT, Davies P, Hamidi-Manesh L. Cyberchondriacs. Int J Adolesc Med Health. 2006 Apr-
Jun; 18(2):209-13.

6. Powell. J and Aileen Clarke. The British Journal of Psychiatry (2006) 189: 273-277

7. Available at: http://www.aihw.gov.au/publications/index.cfm/title/10357

Accessed on September 02, 2006

8. Robine J, Romieu I & Cambois E 1999. Health expectancy indicators. Bulletin of the World Health
Organization 77(2):181 5.

9. Heathcote C, Davis B, Puza B & O Neill T 2003. The health expectancies of older Australians. Journal of Population Research 20(2):169 85.

10. Banks, J. Marmot, M., Oldfield, Z., Smith, JP. Disease and Disadvantage in the United States and in England JAMA. 2006; 295:2037-2045

11. Ruggeri, J. Population Aging, Health Care Spending and Sustainability: Do we really have a crisis? Caledon Institute of Social Policy Paper. September 2002. Available at:

http://pdfdl.oceighty.net/pdf2html.php?url=http://www.caledoninst.org/PDF/553

820274.pdf#search=%22health%20spending%20and%20health%20quality%22 Accessed on September 02, 2006

12. Available at:

http://www.medicalnewstoday.com/medicalnews.php?newsid=50600 Accessed on September 3, 2006

13. Available at: http://www.rand.org/news/press.05/09.14.html Accessed on September 3, 2006

14. Available at: http://www.healthcareitnews.com/story.cms?id=5218

Accessed on September 3, 2006

15. Available at:

http://www.oecd.org/document/37/0,2340,en_2649_37407_36986213_1_1_1_37407

,00.html

Accessed on September 3, 2006

16. Available at: http://www.usmedicine.com/dailyNews.cfm?dailyID=293 Accessed on September 03, 2006

17. Cutler, DM. Rosen, AB., and Vijan, S. The Value of Medical Spending in the United States, 1960-2000. New England Journal of Medicine Volume 355:920- 927August 31, 2006 Number 9 Available at: http://www.news.harvard.edu/gazette/2006/09.15/99-

healthcare.html Accessed on September 4, 2006

18. Thorpe, K.E., and Howard, D.H. The Rise in Spending Among Medicare Beneficiaries: The Role of Chronic Disease Prevalence and Changes in Treatment Intensity. Health Affairs, doi: 10.1377/ hlthaff.25.w378 (Published online August 22, 2006)

Promoting Healthcare ICT Adoption Among Doctors

The leisurely adoption of healthcare information and communication technologies by the health sector is legendary, in contradistinction to its seemingly frenetic pace of information generation. It is also counterintuitive that this is the case considering the growing awareness even in the health industry of the many benefits of these technologies to both healthcare delivery and in curtailing its costs. This is more so that many countries worldwide are feeling the strain of ever-increasing healthcare spending guzzling significant portions of their gross domestic product (GDP), with no end apparently in sight. The reasons for the slowness of the health sector to embrace these technologies are legion. They range from the mundane, for example, veiled or manifest Luddism, to the genuine, such as the costs of some of these technologies, even to the scary, for example the apocalyptic, grey goo doomsday ecophagia theory with self- replicating nanobots amok on our planet that some have postulated. Yet, there are compelling reasons why the health industry cannot afford to continue to treat the adoption of these technologies with levity. Besides the moral implications of repeated reports of flaws regarding patient safety, the burden of disease thereof is significant in many respects1, 2. Public interest in the subject has intensified, in the U.S for examples with key studies such as those in Colorado/Utah and in New York, revealing adverse-events rates of 2.9%, and 3.7% of hospitalizations, 6.6% and 13.6% resulting in deaths, respectively3, 4, 5, with over 50% of these adverse events due to preventable medical errors. Extrapolation of the findings of the former and latter studies respectively to the more than 33.6 million admissions to U.S. hospitals in 1997 showed that at least 44,000 and up to 98,000 American deaths annually due to medical errors3. Estimates of costs to the U.S in lost income and lost household productivity, in disability, and in health care costs of these preventable adverse events were between $17 billion and $29 billion, health care costs, more than 50% of these total costs6, 7. Medical errors also compromise patients faith in the health system, and their doctors in their competence to deliver qualitative health services. For society, diminished/lost workforce productivity, children s poor school attendance, and overall health are not often dismissible costs. In the Institute of Medicine s (IOM) 2000 To Err Is Human report, the IOM Quality of Health Care in America Committee, formed in June 1998 to develop a strategy that will lead to progress in care quality over the next decade, made a number of important proposals on ensuring patient safety, part of an overall quality improvement push. Among these proposals were mandatory, nationwide adverse events reporting, and the implementation of a culture of safety in healthcare organizations with a focus of workforce and processes on making healthcare delivery safer and more reliable. Incomplete access to patient information by multiple healthcare providers, deficient incentive to healthcare providers by third -party buyers to deploy safety and quality measures, minimal attention to medical errors prevention, worsened by fear of scrutiny, itself often due to that of litigation, are some of the issues contributory to the high rates of medical errors. No doubt, medical errors are not restricted to the U.S. Indeed, a survey that the Commonwealth Fund conducted between March and June 2005, of persons with health problems in six countries, namely Canada, the U.K., the U.S., Australia, New Zealand, and Germany showed8 that Canadian patients reported approximately the same medical errors rates as those in the U.S., 30% and 34%, respectively, versus 22% in the U.K. The survey also indicated that Canadians and Americans, 23% and 30%, respectively were less likely to receive same/next-day access to their doctors, versus New Zealand for example, where 58% reported same-day access, the quickest, Germany next, 56%. To underscore the tenacity of the patient safety issue and the need to confront it with even more vigor, a new IOM report released on July 20, 2006 titled showed that medication errors, some of the commonest medical errors, continue to injure 1.5 million persons yearly in the U.S. The estimated additional costs of treating drug-related injuries in just hospitals were up to $3.5 billion annually, less lost wages and productivity or sundry care costs9. Among the recommendations that the committee that wrote the report made were measures to improve communication and interactions between health care professionals and patients, and those by patients for self-protection, the establishment of novel, healthcare consumer-focused information portals, and e- prescribing by 2010 and measures to improve medication naming, labeling, and packaging to lessen confusion and avert errors. It is clear that implementing these recommendations would involve significant healthcare ICT input, and the concerted efforts of all healthcare stakeholders. Committee co-chair Linda R. Cronenwett, dean and professor, School of Nursing, University of North Carolina, Chapel Hill indeed, noted, The frequency of medication errors and preventable adverse drug events is cause for serious concern We need a comprehensive approach to reducing these errors that involves not just health care organizations and federal agencies, but the industry and consumers as well. So did the comments of co-chair J. Lyle Bootman, dean and professor, College of Pharmacy, University of Arizona,Tucson, that Our recommendations boil down to ensuring that consumers are fully informed about how to take medications safely and achieve the desired results, underline the issues at the core of patient safety. Furthermore, his comment also th at, Health care providers have the tools and data necessary to prescribe, dispense, and administer drugs as safely as possible and to monitor for problems. The ultimate goal is to achieve the best care and outcomes for patients each time they take a medication, are instructive, in particular regarding the direction of healthcare delivery in an era of increasing public awareness of the value of health and of the sophistication of their expectations of health services delivery vis-à-vis the increasing consumer-centricity of healthcare delivery. In other words, that we would have to be more quality-conscious regarding healthcare delivery is no longer in doubt. In fact, it is imperative, as is doctors being active participants in the process. Considering that healthcare delivery, as outcome, is the culmination of the intercalation of a variety of issues with underlying sub-issues and processes both health and non-health related, dynamic and static factors in turn at play in determining the nature, extent and outcomes of these interactions, change is not only implicit but inevitable in the overall outcome. In other words, healthcare delivery is a product of an inevitable and enduring process of change hence could never be perfect at any point in the change process. This means that we need to recognize potential quality degraders in the health system, and prevent their development or abort their manifestation. How else could we do this other than engaging in a continuous quality appraisal and improvement exercise in the health system as a whole?

Does this therefore not imply the implementation of the technologies and other measures that would enable the realization of the delivery of qualitative health services on an ongoing basis, such as those recommended by the committees mentioned above? Would it not even be more rational to achieve this objective simultaneously reducing health spending, in other words, for any health system to aim to achieve these dual healthcare delivery objectives? The report on medications errors mentioned earlier noted on the average at least one medication error per hospital patient per day and 1.5 million preventable injuries annually, 400,000, and 800,000 preventable drug-related injuries annually in hospitals, and long-term care settings, respectively, costs of the former alone, $3.5 billion in extra medical costs in 2006. The rates of preventable drug-related injuries just among outpatient clinic Medicare recipients were about 530,000, extra medical costs in 2000 for these patients, according to one study, about $887 million, these costs and those aforementioned less lost wages and productivity, among other costs. Is it not ironical that health systems would be incurring such financial costs, not to mention the burden of increased morbidity and mortality that ought to, in the main be seeking ways to reduce health spending and improve the quality of healthcare delivery? Should healthcare organizations and providers not therefore heed the committee s recommendations regarding improving patient safety, which as we earlier noted would no doubt involve healthcare ICT playing key roles in implementing?

Should all concerned therefore not actively promote the adoption and implementation of these technologies by doctors and other healthcare providers on the one hand, and healthcare consumers on the other, considering the important bidirectional information flow crucial to achieving patient safety, among other major components of healthcare delivery quality? Indeed, the committee also recommended not just strengthening the patient-provider partnership, but also the use of incentives to align the pursuit of patient safety with profitability of hospitals, healthcare providers, pharmacies, manufacturers, insurance firms, and others, to buoy the business justification for quality and patient safety. any would ascribe readily the pervasive information asymmetry in the health sector, in particular between doctors and their patients to an atavistic paternalism inherent in the dyadic, an asymmetry in which sense, they would argue that the former has a moral obligation to redress. Regardless, the average healthcare consumer still trusts his/her doctor to provide accurate and current health information, including about their drug regimens, and about clinically significant medication errors that occurred, harmful or otherwise, tasks the former need to take even more seriously considering the findings on medical/ medication-error rates and their costs mentioned above. Would the deployment of the appropriate healthcare software and other ICT not facilitate the achievement of these tasks, particularly in tandem with that by healthcare consumers with which those of their providers could interface seamlessly, for examples, electronic medical records (EMR) and personal health records (PHR)? Could these technologies not also interface with the health information network of a particular healthcare jurisdiction, at the local, state/ provincial, even national levels, with for example both provider and consumer able to receive the information they need, targeted and contextualized, or access it via a dedicated web site such as one by the National Library of Medicine (NLM)? There are many different medical and related databases for doctors, some free, others commercial, some web-based, others usable on stationary and/or mobile devices, where they could obtain current information on medications, their side effects, and interactions with other medications, among others, and information on diagnosis and treatment of medical conditions. There are also a number of websites and databases that cater to the health information needs of the public, the proposal of the committee mentioned earlier that the NLM in the U.S. ought to be the principal organization for providing online health resources for the public, clear information regarding drugs, indicative of the gravity of the information asymmetry issue. It did not only recommend that NLM does so via a Web site that would be a hub of all-inclusive, objective, and clear drug information dissemination, but also that it should collaborate with others to appraise online health information, designating Web sites with current and accurate content, and with FDA, and CMS, to establish a national network of telephone helplines. These helplines would enable persons who lack access to and cannot comprehend printed health information due to illiteracy, language and other difficulties, to obtain and report medication errors and related issues. We should note, however, that significant issues regarding health information dissemination exist and require our urgent attention. The findings of a recent report that showed that the contents of the admittedly significant amount of data, health information, and services available online by state-run health departments nonetheless in the main, are not only way above the comprehension level of the average American, but also are not accessible to persons with disabilities and non-English speakers are telling10. According to the authors of the report published in the Journal of Health Care for the Poor and Underserved, Brown University researchers Darrell M. West and Edward Alan Miller, Inaccessible websites hurt the underprivileged and make it difficult to justify the investment in technology that has taken place in state governments around the country Unless these concerns are addressed, public e-health will remain the domain of highly educated and affluent individuals who speak English and do not suffer from physical impairments. This underscores the point about the persistence and pervasiveness of information asymmetry that we need to rectify and in doing which doctors have a crucial role to play. The authors observed that the majority of state governments-run public health websites did not have contents written at the eight-grade level at which 50% of Americans read, that in fact just 20% had contents written at that level in 2005, 62%, written at the 12th grade level that year. They also noted that in the same year, 58% of the state sites failed to meet the minimum accessibility standards disability advocates recommended, for examples, speech synthesizers/Braille displays-capable text, and procedures for utilizing Text Telephones (TTY)/ Telecommunications Devices for the Deaf (TDD). They also lacked specific software to aid mobility- impaired persons navigate intricate databases and documents, via for examples, voice commands or eye motion. Additionally, the authors noted that only 10% of these websites offered any non -English materials in 2000, although English translation levels increased to 32% and 44% in 2003 and 2004, respectively, but fell to 34% in 2005. Progress, in bridging the access gap seems to be inching ahead but could, and should no doubt be faster, were we to achieve quicker, the dual healthcare delivery goals that is undeniably crucial to not just the U.S. health systems but also those of other countries worldwide. As the authors rightly noted, Unless websites are configured in such a way that all Americans can share in the benefits of new technology, the advantages of the Internet in terms of information and service availability will be denied to those unable to take advantage of conventional online resources. There could be no gainsaying the significance of rectifying health information asymmetry and of the need for accessibility to health services by all, considering the increasing emphasis in many health systems on patient-centeredness, and its importance to the healthcare consumer becoming more discerning in his/her perception of a variety of health related issues including service utilization. The more rational use of preventive and curative services alike would no doubt improve the overall health and well-being of the populace and reduce health spending, even if on the aggregate in the long term. It is therefore in the interest of all to encourage the access to and acquisition of current and accurate health information by, in particular, doctors, who are we noted earlier many patients still trust as their best sources of information on health issues. Many healthcare organizations, and doctors, indeed have their web sites, which they also need to ensure meet the requirements we have so far mentioned to make the websites more accessible to all healthcare consumers. However, doctors could also provide information verbally or via healthcare information and communication technologies in a variety of other ways, for example, via emails, sending links to articles they consider would benefit their patients, or indeed, the actual articles in a variety of multimedia formats, even writing/sending articles themselves on topical health issues via emails, or PHR, among others. The authors also observed that an increase in privacy and security policies among state sites, with just 8% and 4% of health departments having online privacy policy and security policy, respectively in 2000, whereas in 2005, 86% and 62%, again, respectively, did, attributable to efforts to implement Title II of the Health Insurance Portability and Accountability Act (HIPAA). This is also an issue that doctors need to bear in mind, as their efforts to communicate and share health information with their patients, for example via PHR integrated with the physicians health information systems would doubtless improve, the more guarantee they give on the safety and security of patients information.

The need for such avenues for bidirectional information exchange between the healthcare provider/ organizations and the consumer on drug use and associated problems, and indeed the provider/ consumer encounter overall, is not just important in contemporary healthcare delivery, but becomes urgent in a milieu plagued with many system and other issues, to resolve which doctors would be ever more pivotal. Many health jurisdictions for example recognize the need for them to embrace the dual healthcare delivery objectives11. It makes sense to be able to deliver qualitative healthcare for less money. Yet, many are still stuck with paper-based information systems, despite studies showing that these systems result in higher medical error rates, and that deploying computerized reporting systems, for example, result in a fall in adverse drug events (ADEs), according to one research study by almost 300%, cost of data collection yearly also less substantially12,13. There is no doubt that some are implementing a variety of healthcare information and communication technologies for examples, electronic medical records (EMR), computerized physician order entry (CPOE), bar coding, web-based reporting, even e- prescribing, to improve patient safety14, but the pace of healthcare ICT adoption doubtless remains painfully slow. This is despite that several studies have indicated that these technologies help reduce medical/medication error rates and improve patient safety15. That many doctors write illegibly is well known, and that this could create readability issues, some with potential lethal consequences for the patient who could end up receiving the wrong medication or dosage simply stands to reason. Why then, one would wonder a health jurisdiction, doctor, or healthcare organization, would not implement e-prescribing for example, which not only eliminates problems with handwriting legibility but, combined with decision-support tools, could alert the doctor doing the prescribing, automatically, to possible drug/drug and other interactions, and allergies, among other problems-in-waiting? There is a myriad of possible reasons, costs key not to mention and in particular, in alliance with the demoralization of integrating the disparate legacy information systems many find themselves stuck with, but which merely literally sucks funds in maintenance and license fees barely, still value-added, the incentive to acquire more healthcare could hardly be robust. This example highlights some of the many system issues, some regulatory, others relating to reimbursement, yet others to certification, hindering the adoption of healthcare ICT and on which urgent attention is crucial, to achieve the recommendation, for example, of the committee referred to earlier that all healthcare providers should have plans in place by 2008 to e-prescribe. The committee indeed, also recommended they should all be so doing by 2010 and that all pharmacies ought to be able to receive prescriptions electronically by then. Less than 20% of doctors in the U.S. e- prescribe, and some state laws still ban the exercise altogether. South Carolina s Board of Pharmacy for example, reportedly denied SureScripts, a pharmacy consortium that advances e-prescribing, approval in 2005, and as a spokesman for the board put it, electronic prescribing is only permissible if it goes directly from the doctor s office to the pharmacy of the patient s choice Most e- prescribing companies that have come before the board send the e-prescribing through a routing company, citing the board s concern regarding confidentially and security issues16. The report however, pointed out that the board has sent recommendations to the South Carolina Legislature that would allow e- prescribing technology with a routing configuration but the routing firm must obtain the board s permission. In Wyoming, the issues are slightly different as the digital signature format in use to identify authorized prescriber poses significant technological challenges than the more commonly used electronic signature format, which itself highlights another important obstacle in the way of e-prescribing, that of e-prescribing standards. The Medicare Modernization Act of 2003, among other recent developments though has eased the process by which many states in the U.S. would approve regulations that would allow e- prescribing. As if the technical issues regarding e prescribing are not enough, integrating formulary into these technologies, which would link providers, payers, pharmacies, and the healthcare consumer, which would, in particular with the consumer involved, be the epitome of the conceptual underlay of electronic data interchange, from the perspective of institutional economics. In short, it is when we would begin to take issues regarding transaction costs seriously, as we really should. Is it any wonder then that the CMS is mandating e-prescribing for health plans that provide Medicare health plan products, and does this not speak to the need to expedite efforts at establishing form ulary and e-prescribing standards? In the U.S., Medicare Part D is also a major driver of e- prescribing technologies, which experts tip to be standard practice in the years ahead, including their nature and scope, and their adoption. So is the underlying assumption by experts and the governments in the country and in others such as Canada, and the U.K., that e-prescribing is the prelude toward large scale adoption of electronic health records (EHR) technologies, which vendors continue to enrich with versatile e-prescribing capabilities, facilitating the buy-in of decision makers, hence buoying their acquisitions. In the U.S., 48 states now allow e prescribing, or have legislation in the making to allow its use, interoperability, and transactions standards rigorously pursued, as are incentives for their adoption. Canada and the U.K., and other developed countries are also following suit. As with the other healthcare information and communication technologies, the challenges to e prescribing are however, multifaceted. E-prescribing, viewed in the context of not just the transactional costs of information exchange, but also their theoretical underpinnings in emergent institutional economics, underscores the need for a continual approach to rectifying related but equally important issues such as information asymmetry crucial to assuring patient safety. In other words, we need to acknowledge the ongoing need for the collaboration of different stakeholders at various levels for the evolution of the necessary institutional structures both at the public and private levels that would ensure the bidirectional information flow mentioned earlier. Such flow of information would in addition to empowering the public not just on issues relating to their health, but also healthcare purchasers on ensuring the receipt of appropriate healthcare, and curtailing its abuse. The result in both cases would be the delivery of qualitative healthcare simultaneously curtailing healthcare costs. When professional organizations emerge for exam ple, certifying and regulating healthcare provision, or not-for- profit accreditation bodies such as the Electronic HealthCare Network Accreditation Commission (EHNAC), which only recently concluded its e- prescribing Accreditation Criteria, expand its mandate into pharmacy networks and aggregators collaborating with over twenty e-prescribing industry representatives, institutional evolution becomes manifest. The example of EHNAC, which seeks to accredit bodies, for examples, payers, providers, clearinghouses, transactions processors, value-added networks (VANs), and provider management organizations, which send/receive HIPAA regulated transactions, or that transport/process EDI transactions between two or more trading partners in the health sector, using criteria to incorporate the highest quality measures specifically focused on e-prescribing transactions is instructive. This is so as it not only sets high transaction standards, in this case for e- prescribing, but also plans to review, consider, and incorporate as need be in its next version of its e-prescribing criteria, the federal e-prescribing regulations when adopted eventually. This exemplifies the potential for cross-institutional collaboration that would typify progress in healthcare delivery in the years ahead, whose result would facilitate the achievement of the dual healthcare delivery goals. That transaction costs guzzles significant portions of the gross domestic product (GDP) of many developed countries is not in doubt, more intricate transactions such as those involved in healthcare delivery incurring potentially even more costs, both ex-ante, for example in determining the provision of and securing contractual agreements for services and goods, and ex- post, appraising/supervising the contract, am ong others. These issues make the potential to reduce the costs, while still delivering qualitative health services an attractive proposition, and stresses why the increasing adoption of the technologies such as healthcare ICT, which would help in so doing is inevitable in the health sector, and indeed, in related areas such as the health insurance industry. Doctors would no doubt be part of this transition, and would indeed, need to play a major role in the process considering that they generate a significant quantity of the information exchange, a key transaction entity, not to mention their professional and other obligations to support efforts by all stakeholders toward the realization of the dual healthcare delivery goals.

To be sure, doctors are not oblivious to increasing interests in the use of healthcare information and communication technologies in the delivery of health services. In fact, many are actively involved in promoting healthcare ICT. With e- prescribing technologies alone implemented in the U.S., nationwide estimated to save up to $30 billion yearly in health spending alone, for example, not even the costs of these technologies would prevent its widespread adoption, with insurers, among others, funding initiatives across the U.S., expecting savings from their investments in these technologies to curtail costs in the long term 17. Doctors in many developed countries have also begun to implement e- prescribing technologies in increasing numbers, as they are in fact progressively embracing healthcare ICT in general. The Canadian government has infused over a billion dollars in the past couple of years into Canada Health Infoway to spearhead the development of healthcare ICT in the country, electronic health records technologies, key such technologies. Employers and insurers now more and more prefer healthcare providers that utilize healthcare ICT to those that do not, in countries such as the U.S. In British Columbia, the province s physicians published a document, titled, Getting It Right, patient centred information technology , a discussion paper in January 2004, essentially advocating more use of these technologies in healthcare delivery18. The document among others, expressed the vision of the province s medical association (BCMA) as, That practicing physicians take a leading role in supporting the development of affordable, integrated, and easy to use information systems that provide physicians with accurate, secure, complete and timely information to enhance the quality of patient care and increase practice efficiency . There is no doubt about the recognition by the association that healthcare ICT could help in achieving major healthcare delivery goals such as the dual healthcare delivery objectives mentioned earlier, as increased efficiency and healthcare delivery quality improvement are the basic ingredients of costs saving. There is therefore burgeoning interests in the use of healthcare ICT across board. However, and as the BCMA document revealed, promoting the adoption of healthcare information and communication technologies among doctors remains a critical issue that needs urgent attention. As we noted earlier, it is likely that efforts to incorporate these technologies into mainstream medical practice and healthcare delivery overall would likely come to naught without the active engagement of some of its most intense end users. The BC doctors for example noted their lack of involvement in a variety of healthcare ICT projects in the province such as PathNET and the Electronic Medical Summary (e-MS) project through the Vancouver Island Health Authority. They acknowledged the Information Management/Information Technology (IM/IT) workshop government hosted in collaboration with the BCMA in September 2003, but urged more such efforts, a clear indication of the doctors desire to participate in the inevitable advance toward an e-health age that other doctors elsewhere need also embrace. A 2003 survey of BC s practicing physicians, 4195 physicians in all, 47% of them GPs and family doctors, on information systems showed that doctors appreciated the significance of healthcare ICT for examples EMRs, pharmaceutical and laboratory information systems in qualitative and efficient healthcare delivery. However, the BCMA in recognizing the potential benefits of healthcare ICT was quick to point out that, major issues and challenges remain that need urgent attention in order to develop an integrated, province-wide healthcare ICT infrastructure, two crucial obstacles being to ensure patient information privacy, and that doctors could afford healthcare ICT. There is no doubt about the need to address these issues and challenges, but e need first to determine what they are, as the BC doctors did for their own jurisdiction. In other words, the obstacles in the way of doctors implementing healthcare ICT are not universal. Even when costs, to which many would ascribe their slowness in embracing these technologies, or some other obstacles, seem to cut across countries, on scrutiny, the elements of these costs issues would likely differ from one jurisdiction to the next, even within the same country. Thus, the need of the doctors, and the most appropriate means to meet them would be different depending on the jurisdiction in question. The point remains though that we must determine what these issues are, and one way to do so is to engage in an analytical exercise involving at first, high-level determination of the issues involved in the particular healthcare delivery challenge, in this case the adoption by doctors, of healthcare information and communication technologies. Consequent upon this determination, are the decomposition and exposition of these issues, in a continuous process that would reveal underlying issues and processes attendance to which, barring any historical fallacies, would result in the achievement of the desired objective, namely, the promotion of healthcare ICT deployment and use by doctors and indeed, other healthcare providers. It is therefore crucial for any effort to accelerate the deployment of these technologies in healthcare delivery, an essential element of our quest to achieve the dual healthcare delivery goals, to recognize the need for such an in-depth analytical exercise, a process cycle analysis, of the issues and challenges confronting doctors in the widespread diffusion of the technologies. Patient-centered healthcare delivery for example, is becoming commonplace in many countries. Implicit in this model of care is adherence to strict quality standards, which many believe requires the commitment at a high level, by providers of care to deliver. The implications of this are wide-ranging for not just the outcome of the healthcare delivery process, but along the way towards achieving this goal. In other words, we need to revisit reimbursement schemes for doctors as part of our efforts to secure this commitment, which would encompass investing in the appropriate healthcare ICT to facilitate its realization. Pay-for-performance (P4P) is a reimbursement model, which could as many contend ensure that doctors deliver the qualitative healthcare that patient-centred healthcare delivery mandates while simultaneously reducing healthcare costs, compared to, for example, the fee-for- service model, which many argue actually increases health spending without concomitantly guaranteeing qualitative healthcare delivery. However, even P4P has been under intense scrutiny lately regarding its ability to deliver on its promises, literally, besides various other issues such as the difficulty in determining the appropriate reimbursement for whom, and for what performance . This is not to mention the suggestion that self-referral particularly with the emergence in recent times of high-powered, specialty clinics and hospitals would distort market operations, and interfere with the accomplishment in full, of the P4P model s potential. There is indeed, indication that P4P is improving performance, hence the quality of healthcare delivery, for examples, as shown in recent reports on U.K s P4P scheme, the United Kingdom s Quality and Outcomes Framework (QOF) for general practitioners (GPs)19. U.K GPs have no doubt performed better, but the health authorities reportedly paid much more than budgeted for it. In the QOF s first year, GPs scored a mean of 91% compliance with clinical guidelines, which means an extra $700 million in additional physician costs, past the $1.8 billion in new funds, a 20% rise in the U.K. s NHS family practice expenditure and 30% of GPs incomes, already in the QOF s budget. The result: zero new funds in QOF s current iteration, and a rise in the baseline levels benchmarks for appraising GPs performance quality. These figures attest to the fact that P4P could work in achieving the dual healthcare delivery goals, but that it needs appropriate tweaking based on the peculiarities of a particular health jurisdiction. As parts of its efforts to improve the quality of healthcare delivery in the country, the U.K government in 1998, developed clinical guidelines, an inspection process, and a number of quality improvement measures in doctors offices. It also developed a set of mainly nonpecuniary incentives, for examples, providing doctors with performance feedbacks, and releasing performance information to peers and, less so, the public. It is hardly an issue thus, that the GPs performance was so good although we should aim for full marks in particular with exception reporting, permitted. What is even more contentious is the fact that the government seems to be paying more, increasing health spending, in effect, as many contend, for services doctors already provide, based on the underestimated performance benchmarks used. This is no doubt a lesson that other countries implementing P4P need to imbibe, and one that points to the need for doctors to embrace and implement value-added healthcare information and communication technologies that would enable them deliver even higher levels of care, the overall effect of which would be positive for the entire health system in the long term.

In the health system's part, it needs to determine the benchmark levels for its GPs and family doctors based on criteria most appropriate to their practice milieu, and do the same for each specialist service. In other words, it would be pointless to expect GPs to have certain technologies when the technical infrastructures are not in place in that environment for these technologies to work. On the other hand, it would be appropriate to encourage them to implement and use those technologies that they could to improve both preventive and curative services, and reward them for initiatives in healthcare ICT deployment even ahead of the proposed technological resources of the health jurisdiction. For examples it should reward the use of EMR, wireless, and web-based technologies that w ould enhance healthcare delivery even before the jurisdiction s EHR technologies become fully functional. Some have suggested delaying payments of incentives until a year after baseline measurements to avert such unanticipated reimbursements as the UK did, or as in the U.S., construing P4P as a zero-sum game with no new funds on hand, a measured approach that would engender solid baseline benchmarks. It is also important to ensure that doctors focus on the quality measures rather than on treating the patient, which would require double-checking with the healthcare consumer not only his/her satisfaction ratings of the encounter, but also whether he/she noticed overly focus by the provider on any of the quality indicators. This again underscores the need for widespread healthcare ICT diffusion as these technologies could enable such tripartite communication pathways and indeed, make the financial consequences of such patient interviews/surveys more rational and measurable. There are of course many other ways to encourage doctors to adopt healthcare ICT, offering them other incentives besides via P4P. Examples include free trial software, opportunities for payments in instalments, licensing incentives, funds by government or others to purchase software, free technical assistance in software installation and reduced maintenance costs, free software upgrades at least for a defined period, and other reduced payments for products and services including networking and hardware. In other words, an important aspect of the promotion of healthcare ICT use among doctors is making the technologies more affordable, that is reducing not just costs to acquire them, but in fact, the total costs of ownership. The often-high costs of healthcare ICT is a major reason many doctors, even those that want to implement these technologies, are not able to do so, and why those that do often do not implement all the features of those technologies that they purchase, hence are unable to benefit from them in full. This inability to exploit these technologies maximally partly explains the findings in some studies that cast doubts on the potential of healthcare ICT to help in the achievement of the dual healthcare delivery goals mentioned above20. Another key problem doctors have with healthcare information technologies is that they complain that these technologies slow down the performance of their everyday healthcare delivery tasks, compromising productivity, an undesirable situation as this ultimately negates efforts to achieve the dual healthcare delivery goals20. Thus, software vendors and other healthcare ICT firms also need to ensure that these technologies have user-friendly interfaces, are easy to operate, and that they facilitate rather than hinder productivity. They should ensure that the learning curves for their products are anything but steep, and should be involved actively in facilitating training in the use of these technologies, prior to their purchase and on an ongoing basis, in particular as new major updates emerge, a service that could offer competitive advantage to these firms. There is no doubt that these incentives are worth the while across board, as the more doctors implement these technologies, the likelier would be the cumulative benefits reverberate in all theatres of the healthcare delivery enterprise, and new research continues to support this assertion. A recent analysis for example, based on data from the Hospital Quality Incentive Demonstration project in the U.S, a government- private sector pay-for-performance collaborative effort operated by Premier Inc. healthcare alliance and the Center for Medicare & Medicaid Services indicated that adherence to quality measures in patient management resulted not just in saving lives, but also costs, in four of five diseases21. Indeed, on applying the findings from the 250 hospitals involved in the project to those in the entire country, there would be an estimated 5,700 less deaths and up to $1.35 billion annual healthcare costs savings. Incidentally, the researchers stressed that more- widespread adoption such evidence-based approaches call for healthcare organizations to utilize healthcare ICT, which could make healthcare guidelines and patient information available at the point of care (POC.) Furthermore, with the treatment of pneumonia, heart bypass, heart attack, and hip and knee replacement, conditions in which quality measures were effective, the wider application of these measures say in 2004, would have led to almost 5,700, 8,100, 10,000, and 750,000 fewer deaths, complications, re-admissions and hospital days, respectively. Earlier analyses of the treatment of pneumonia and coronary artery bypass graft procedures had indicated similar results, as had those of heart attack and hip and knee replacement procedures21. That such analyses conducted for care process improvement for the treatment of patients with chronic heart failure indicated an increase in healthcare costs21, however, points to the complexity of the issues involved in certain instances of the application of these technologies to healthcare delivery, such as the tendency for more service utilization, including for the prescription of more interventions. In some cases, as some could contend, some doctors might even be managing to meet the quality measures that result in performance-related reimbursements. There is therefore a need for better understanding of the issues involved in the applications of these technologies in the treatment of chronic health conditions, the tendency for more than one clinician to be involved in the management of which further complicates the situation. Nonetheless, as these are important aspects of the overall efforts to encourage the implementation of these technologies by doctors, and indeed, other healthcare professionals, and stakeholders, teasing out these issues is paramount. This also underscores the points made earlier about the value of process cycle analyses in the healthcare delivery enterprise, where in fact through decomposition/exposition exercises of these issues would h elp clarify them, and reveal the solutions to addressing them effectively. Being in the highest 20% in documented adherence to evidence-based care guidelines in the project mentioned above, entitles participating hospitals to extra Medicare reimbursement. Such incentives would no doubt encourage the implementation of healthcare ICT, which would in turn help with compliance with quality standards, and facilitate the achievement of the dual healthcare delivery objectives. The recent report by the U.S., Health and Human Services Secretary Michael Leavitt to Congress on plans to advance the Medicare Quality Improvement Organization program highlights this point22. This report, essentially follows the IOM studies mentioned earlier, and re-emphasizes the significance of healthcare ICT adoption in improving care for Medicare recipients, and indeed, for all healthcare consumers. According to the Secretary, CMS is committed to promoting the use of health information technology by providers and the specification of qu ality measures such that they can be reported from electronic systems and to harmonizing such activities with the developing National Health Information Network . He added regarding Medicare s QIO Program that it is is supporting one of the largest national efforts to provide help to physician offices in adoption of health information technology, and its use in improving care and reporting clinical quality measures. The agency is also encouraging hospitals and other providers to adopt health information technology that will allow for reporting of clinical quality data. There is no doubt about the need for other countries and health jurisdictions to establish similar programs in order to enhance their prospects of achieving the dual healthcare delivery goals, but also none about the need to take the recommendations of the IOM committee that prepared the 2006 IOM study mentioned earlier to heart, literally. The committee had noted that quality improvement organizations (QIOs), private entities Medicare contracted to improve the quality of services that healthcare organizations and doctors provide, should concentrate on technical assistance provision on quality improvement rather than the supervisory/regulatory role they currently play. In other words, that they should be more involved in providing healthcare consumers with quality and pricing data and information, a crucial element in helping them to be more discerning in making healthcare delivery choices, and assisting doctors and other health providers in their efforts to adopt healthcare ICT.

In keeping with these recommendations, the Secretary noted the plan to access the effects of QIOs on improving Medicare quality, improve financial oversight and governance to ensure the proper use of contract funds, increase competition for QIO contracts, and improve the prospects of QIOs performing better at the local level. As we noted earlier, it is in fact apt that even P4P, should to take local flavors regarding issues surrounding quality appraisals and remuneration into consideration, hence the need as the Secretary noted to boost QIOs performance at this level, among others. Indeed, it is crucial for such organizations to focus in particular on the adoption of healthcare information and communication technologies by doctors and healthcare providers as parts of their quality improvement efforts, considering the immense benefits to healthcare delivery derivable from these technologies. As the 2006 IOM report s lead author and committee chair Steven Schroeder, Distinguished Professor of Health and Health Care, University of California, San Francisco, noted, We believe that the care provided to Medicare beneficiaries has improved too slowly and that QIOs should concentrate on accelerating these improvements. While w e recognize the importance of the proper handling of beneficiary complaints and case reviews, these organizations have not yet realized their full potential to help health care providers meet the highest quality standards. The role of QIOs should be to imp rove health care practice rather than to supervise or regulate it. There is also therefore, an element of urgency in these issues that we cannot ignore, even as QIOs redirect their activities, considering the financial implications of the slowness in the widespread diffusion and implementation of healthcare ICT, which soaring health spending in many countries exemplify, and the burden of disease and illness with potentially significant consequences for overall health. That seniors and others individuals with higher incomes, will be paying higher Medicare premiums than other recipients will in 2007, part of efforts by government to ensure the long-term financial viability of Medicare, buttresses this point, the surcharge, which means seniors will not longer pay the same premium , estimated to affect one million to two million recipients. This surcharge, a provision in the 2003 law including a prescription drug benefit to Medicare, would affect persons with incomes over $80,000, and married couples with over $160,000, those with incomes over $200,000, who currently pay a premium of $88.50 a month, will pay four times this amount in 2009. These issues again, bring to the fore the need to curtail healthcare spending while not compromising care quality, and the imp ortance of the appreciation of the role doctors need to play in the achievement of these dual healthcare delivery goals on the one hand, and that of the need for the appropriate measures to encourage them to play this role. Hence the importance of the observation the Secretary made that The QIO Program is using its resources to help providers implement four strategies that can yield high performance: measurement and reporting, adoption and use of health information technology, redesign of care processes, and changes to organizational culture and management, in his report to the U.S. Congress as noted earlier. According to the Secretary, These transformational strategies differ from the incremental changes that QIOs promoted in the past, and are needed if providers are to achieve high performance. The need for such strategies could not be timelier particularly with the re-conceptualization of healthcare information and communication technologies as constitutive rather than be merely facilitative technologies, capable of actually becoming embedded in the processes that culminate in healthcare delivery transforming these processes along a continuous quality improvement spectrum. In fact, doctors and healthcare providers that not only embrace these technologies, but appreciate fully this approach to viewing them would be moving beyond acquiring and implementing what some have termed commoditized technologies, into a different realm, that of potentially differentiating their products and services from their competition. This would no doubt have implications for healthcare-consumer patronage, and by extension, for revenue generation, and this, regardless, of the funding system of the health system. That President Bush on Aug. 22, 2006 issued an executive order requiring federal agencies and their health care contractors to promote the use of interoperable health information technology products, so that data can be easily shared, also supports the increasing realization of the benefits of these technologies to the overall health system. This in fact applies to all other countries, which should therefore, also take necessary measures to foster their adoption by doctors and other healthcare stakeholders, and many indeed, are. Canada Health Infoway for example has assembled major vendors and a provincial partner that would speed up its $100-million plan to create a case management system to help track communicable diseases for examples SARS and the Avian flu in the country, including IBM, which announced on September 07, 2006 that it has a $24 million five-year contract. IBM would lead a group of vendors that build health-information surveillance products, British Columbia's Ministry of Health chosen by Infoway as the official client to implement the system on completion, software created initially for B.C., which other provinces and territories would be able to buy, hence implement their copies, using the same pricing and terms stipulated in B.C. s contract. This would allow adherence to specified standards yet the flexibility required to enable the system to adjust to local processes and requirements24. Canada Health Infoway indeed, has a broader mandate, essentially to implement EHR across the country by 2009 via providing funds and direction to healthcare entities intent on digitalizing patient data management processes. Appropriately integrated, which it should, and which highlights the need for paying attention to the problems stalling interoperability of health information systems, the proposed surveillance system would be able to extract data from these EHRs. However, its intended design would also enable it operate independently, if a health jurisdiction did not yet have an EHR, when client or provider registries could offer the data to the surveillance system, again underlining the point we made earlier about encouraging doctors to implement healthcare ICT even prior to the implementation of certain technical infrastructures in their healthcare jurisdictions. A point further highlighted by the observation of Todd Kalyniuk, a partner in health care with IBM Global Business Services that IBM would develop a module with immunization histories, for example able to track a patient s status based on information GPs input, even have data on lab results. This again stresses the need for us to pursue our efforts to encourage doctors to implement healthcare ICT with renewed vigor in Canada, and indeed, in other countries, not just to ensure that the substantial financial and other investments in this undeniably valu able project, and indeed, healthcare ICT projects in other countries, do not come to naught. Some vendors with products still based on H ealth Level7 version 2x messaging standard, are unhappy about the decision to base the surveillance system on HL7 v. 3.0, although it is important to stick to consistent standards/protocols if we were to ensure the all-important interoperability between invariably disparate provider systems. With regards this issue, Infoway has been examining, since it announced the proposed disease surveillance system in 2005, Public Health Agency of Canada (PHAC) s Public Health Information System (i-PHIS), which tracks a number of different healthcare data/information in seven Canadian jurisdictions. Its conclusion that health authorities used some iPHIS modules but not, and in fact not all similarly, prompted Infoway put its vision in its paper, iPHIS Gold, which includes some aspects of the original system it deemed would be valuable in the new, given to bidders on the proposed system to include in their proposals. The system based on service-oriented architecture will ensure interconnectivity of its copies, its performance managed with IBM s Tivoli software, the system s user interface, developed with IBM s WebSphere Portal software will feature across applications. Thus even with the likelihood of the different commercial off-the shelf software (COTS) the design team would use in its development, and with which the variety of end -users would access it, adherence to these standards and protocols, would facilitate their seamless integration. This would, no doubt, help, by making connectivity and usage easier, promote the acquisition and implementation by doctors, of the software, and other technologies they would need to participate fully in its operations. As Tim Beasley, Infoway program director also noted, the system w ould need to operate in compliance with the various health privacy laws in Canada, a critical issue in the use of healthcare ICT by doctors, and one that incidentally caused consternation among some regarding Infoway choosing B.C. as a partner. This is in view of the latter s Health Ministry s decision to outsource management of it health records to a U.S. firm in 2004, which raised questions about privacy then.

While privacy issues loom large in the healthcare ICT adoption landscape in Canada, and indeed, elsewhere, and their resolution is crucial to promoting the widespread diffusion of these technologies among doctors, there are outstanding issues regarding patient safety in the country that need equal focus. Some have recommended the establishment in Canada of a national patient safety agency25, whose function would be to act, pretty-much as an independent overseer of safety procedures, which others have opposed as being unworkable because provincial governments run health systems in the country26. With 30% of medical treatments complicated with adverse events, and up to 24 000 Canadians dying each year due to medical errors, that a Health Canada-commissioned report recommended that the health care system needs implement a new, proactive, system to prevent medical errors and assure patient safety is hardly surprising26. The country already has the Canadian Patient Safety Institute, and has other national health organizations with nationwide mandates, for example, the Public Health Agency of Canada (PHAC) mentioned earlier, and the Health Council of Canada, which makes the revisiting the mandate of the Safety Institute, much like Secretary Leavitt proposed for QIO to the U.S. Congress mentioned above, conceivable. With magnitude of the problem of safety, not just in Canada, but in the U.S., as we noted above, and indeed, elsewhere, we need indeed, to have a coordinated national mechanism to ensure the compliance with standardized safety regimes across the country. This would indeed, also help promote the acquisition, implementation, and use of healthcare ICT by doctors, in keeping with benchmarks of care to which they would need to adhere. It is important though, to establish clear responsibilities for the agency, lest it turns out to be supervisory and regulatory rather than actually offering technical assistance on the sorts of quality improvement that would ensure patient safety, such as the deployment of relevant healthcare ICT. This would also foster rather than reduce self-regulation by professional associations, an important aspect of the need to nurture the emergence of the appropriate institutions whose collaborative efforts would cumulatively help achieve the desired objectives of improving the quality of care delivery, including assuring patient safety, simultaneously reducing healthcare costs. It would also assure doctors, and other healthcare professionals, of no loss of status or autonomy, or of practice restrictions. These are issues of concern to these professionals. They are also important to securing their cooperation with efforts to improve patient safety, for example, mandatory reporting of adverse events, even with their anonymity guaranteed. With such reporting for example, not just an important element of quality improvement, but also, with such cooperation secured, would likely encourage doctors and other healthcare professionals to implement the healthcare information and communication technologies that are so crucial to performing these tasks efficiently, and effectively, stipulating an assistive role for such a national safety agency is doubtless most appropriate. We need to continue to do whatever we could to encourage doctors to adopt healthcare ICT, and our efforts must consider all the various issues involved in achieving this goal, which as we have seen thus far are indeed, wide-ranging. Regarding costs, for example, no doubt one such key issues, doing so might be in the best interests of the doctors, and their patients, but also of the software and healthcare ICT vendors, which by allowing doctors to pay in installments as noted earlier for example, would be creating new customers, enlarging their market, and increasing revenue generation. Some would even suggest that such firms or individual developers should offer certain products and services free to doctors, at least for a trial period. With the re-emergence and increasing popularity of this advertising model, it is unlikely to be far-fetched to expect its foray into the healthcare domain anytime soon. In Canada, for example, a Sudbury, Ontario- based GP, Dr. Dennis Reich, has developed a Web-based application called Chyma, which is gaining increasing currency among doctors, to help them in workflow scheduling and information communication and sharing, roughly 5,000 doctors currently using the system in Canada to link with key health facilities in Sudbury, North Bay, Brantford and Scarborough, among others. Developed as an add -on to legacy communications systems through the Internet, Chyma s potential utility is extensive, including besides enabling doctors to manage their on-call schedules at multiple sites, in rectifying provider/patient information asymmetry, and in mobilizing emergency response resources such as during an epidemic or natural disasters. According to Dr. Reich, It s difficult for us to get involved in hospital communications systems," says Reich, pointing out that disparate systems such as Novell, Office or Lotus Notes each require separate system set-up and logon IDs So we created a system that allows healthcare professionals to have the same system no matter where they are27 . This system has been particularly useful in helping solve the scheduling problems of health jurisdictions battling physician-shortages issues. Sault Ste Marie, Ont., for example, which has such issues, u tilizes Chyma throughout the city for its 80,000 inhabitants incorporating ten regional health facilities, hospitals and clinics and the police and coroner s office, alleviating its physician shortage by being able to centrally track and coordinate resource utilization, hence optimization, besides being a veritable information portal. According to Julian Piwowarski, manager of ICT at the Sault Ste. Marie Hospital (SSMH), It s a crisis situation here our area is significantly deprived of primary care physicians Most people use hospital emergency for primary care, that's how bad it is. Chyma not onl illustrates how doctors could help develop health information systems, which makes it much easier for their colleagues to adopt, considering that such developers/collaborators would likely understand the doctors needs in more depth, and address them, but also how offering free, easy to use, healthcare ICT could help in the diffusion of these technologies for healthcare delivery. Almost 1800 users, even the elderly and many that have never used a computer, in Sault for example, utilize the system , in the beta testing of which in 2003 SSMH first participated, as an all-inclusive resource for everyone dealing with emergency response, for example. Chyma s three main parts, the electronic directory the first developed in place of the paper phone book, the electronic on-call schedules plus calendar, developed next, and the knowledge base with protocols/policies for 50 categories plus an alert system, are interconnected, with an added au dit trail to guarantee accountability, and offer real-time data and information. The system has had several upgrades over time, and has becom e even more robust, able to handle, scheduling for doctor s rounds, and executive/administrative meetings, among others, and to facilitate communication in a pandemic response, for example. However, the system does not provide home phone numbers, to protect doctors privacy, which again would encourage even more doctors to use it. Considering the possibility of an outbreak of avian flu or any other epidemic/pandemic, even any natural or manmade disaster that would require instantaneous mobilization of medical resources to respond adequately to such emergencies, the need to encourage the development of such technologies, and to promote their adoption by doctors, including offering them gratis, is undeniable. With software magnate Mark Shuttleworth offering free computer open-source software to facilitate the use of computers and Internet access in South Africa, backed by Hewlett-Packard, and governments in Brazil, China, Spain, India and Malaysia already using Linux- based systems, there is no doubt about the role free software would play in healthcare delivery in many of these and other developing countries. However, with Microsoft funding IT centers in 284 of South Africa's municipalities in a project to extend computer use to half a million poor peoples in the country, other competing models abound that indicate interests by different stakeholders in the efforts to promote ICT diffusion, from which healthcare delivery worldwide no doubt would benefit28. It is important though for health jurisdictions to synchronize with these efforts to facilitate the realization of the eventual objectives of delivering qualitative healthcare cost-effectively and efficiently. In Canada, many hospitals still use extemporized e-mail and phone approaches to mobilize personnel, a situation that needs digitalizing were we to be serious about achieving the dual healthcare delivery goals mentioned above, and which indeed, is. Thus, provincial and federal organizations are in different stages of proposed advanced pandemic communications systems development, which, among others, would establish connectivity to patient e-health records, which underscores the need to promote healthcare ICT, for example, personal health records (PHR), across board, including among the public. Concerning preparations for an imminent or potential pandemic for example, it would no doubt be desirable for GPs to know which of his/ her patients have pending immunizations, what these are, and when they are due, and to be able to alert them automatically. Would some form of connectivity between the GP s health ICT, and the patient s PHR, for example, not facilitate such contact or other functions or healthcare delivery activities, and with links by both to such technologies as Chyma, would both not in fact have access to the availability of services, what they are, where to obtain, them, and so on? Could the implementation and use of these technologies not save lives and reduce healthcare costs under such circumstances, and in those of the many other valuable ways in which they are deployable? Still in Canada, several issues are going to continue to influence not just the nature and extent of investments in healthcare ICT by the various health jurisdictions, but also by healthcare providers and other healthcare stakeholders. To be sure, activities are ongoing regarding the implementation of ICT all over the country that bode well for healthcare delivery improvement. Toronto for example recently became, as Ottawa, Fredericton, and Whistler before it, wireless, with the first phase of its Wi-Fi network, termed One Zone ostensibly, the largest Wi-Fi network in the country became operational in early September 2006, with a formal announcement at Toronto Stock Exchange s Broadcast Centre. The service, whose deployment would be in five phases up to the end of 2006, its initial phase to cover span a six-kilometer radius, including Queen Street to Front Street and Church Street to Spadina Avenue, would be available gratis for six months until March 6, 2007, at the end of which it would offer three dissimilar payment plans. These are a pre-paid $29 monthly subscription, a $10 24-hour plan, and a $5 hourly rate. The plan would cover the entire city in three years, Toronto Hydro Telecom recouping the $2 million project unlikely to be problematic, in particular as the project, targeted at corporate and entrepreneurial clients eventually starts to attract healthcare clients who would increasingly find it invaluable for the sort of doctor/patient communications on the go, among others, mentioned earlier. Coupled with flexible pricing, which would likely happen as more firms establish such services, and with the differentiation in value propositions that the ensuing competition would entail, for examples, faster broadband access, enhanced data/information security, and reliability, among others, issues germane to the health sector, and to both doctors, and healthcare consumers embracing these technologies, patronage would likely increase. This would certainly heighten our prospects of achieving the dual healthcare delivery goals. Indeed, other cities in Canada, such as Fredericton offer Wi-Fi services free of charges, setting the stage for competitive forces to operate, with Toronto for example, in competition with Bell Canada, Telus, and Rogers, all private wireless carriers, who might all someday have to compete with even firms offering these services free.

As earlier mentioned, several different issues would also be important in the widespread diffusion of healthcare ICT among doctors, and other healthcare professionals. One such issue is that of the establishment or otherwise of a parallel healthcare system in the country. The 2005, Supreme Court ruling in the Chaoulli-Zeliotis v. Government of Quebec case asserts that Quebec citizens have the right to obtain private insurance to fund medically necessary health care services when wait times are unduly long. It also heightened debate on private versus public care, and focuses attention on healthcare issues such as those regarding accessibility, specifically, hospital wait times. Quebec no doubt has had to comply with the ruling, but many other provinces seem keen to establish a parallel private health system. Even in Alberta, whose Third Way health reform plans, reportedly the province shelved in May 2006, following the vote in April 2006 by the Alberta Conservative caucus not to pursue its plans to allow Albertans to buy private medical insurance or physicians to operate in the public and private health sectors, the matter has resurfaced. In mid -August 2006, the Alberta government released a new document, Getting on with Better Health Care: Health Policy Framework, containing eight of the ten policy directions the provincial government originally proposed and was purportedly dead . In the document, the government intends, among others, to foster team approach to care, develop new reimbursement/ incentives regimes for doctors to improve care quality, expand primary care networks, and to establish novel health-outcomes and quality-appraisal measures, which would all no doubt involve significant healthcare ICT deployment. The document also contains proposals to expand the role of private surgical clinics and delist future medical services, which some construe as endorsing a parallel private health system albeit without specific reference to private payment and to doctors being able to operate in both sectors. Whether doctors end up spending a certain proportion of their time in the public system to protect its integrity and quality, as Dr Lyle Oberg, one of the two main contenders for the province s premiership elections due in fall 2006, or all of it, could have significant effects on the health system in the near future. The dynamics of private healthcare delivery, are qualitatively different from those of the public health system, and so would the drivers of the decision to invest or not, in healthcare ICT. Some of the proposals in the original Alberta framework, which as we noted earlier overlap with the new for examples, team approach to care delivery, primary networks expansion, digitalization of doctors offices, and electronic health records (EHR) implementation, among others, would operate differently in both sectors. For example, the province provides all its doctors funds annually to comp uterize their offices, funds that they would have to provide themselves, or seek elsewhere if they were operating in the private health sector. This means software vendors, and others willing to help might need to focus on this group of doctors in Alberta to complement the province s efforts to promote healthcare ICT adoption among doctors. This again underscores the point we made earlier about the need to consider the local hue of the issues involved in promoting the diffusion of these technologies among doctors and other healthcare professionals. The healthcare ICT needs of both systems would also vary, competitive drivers in the private sector making it imperative for doctors to adopt these technologies to boost their value propositions, increase patronage, and generate more revenue. The pressure to achieve the dual healthcare delivery objectives would principally drive novel approaches to care delivery in the public sector, if it were to survive, as the exodus of patients to the private health sector could make some health jurisdictions increasingly less economically viable. Thus, as Dr John Cowell, CEO of the Health Quality Council of Alberta recently queried regarding the request by the Calgary Health Region for a review of all emergency and urgent-care services following several complaints by the public, Why do people choose to visit hospital emergency departments? Are there categories whose needs might be met better and faster in other settings? There is no doubt about this possibility, for example, in specialized primary care settings, integrated specialty service provision, perhaps even on a mobile or telehealth basis, or by strengthening ambulatory and domiciliary healthcare delivery, again, all of which would require significant healthcare ICT involvement. Debate on the model of service provision is not peculiar to Canada. In the U.S., for example, there is ongoing controversy over the burgeoning of specialty clinics across the country, particularly intense after the decision by CMS in early Sep tember 2006, not to extend a moratorium on approval of new ones. Thus, planning for new specialty hospitals in California, Indiana, Pennsylvania, and Texas, where about one-third of the 130 specialty hospitals in the U.S. are, continues apace, James Grant, executive vice president of National Surgical Hospitals based in Chicago indicating the building of about 30 new specialty hospitals by 2007. While proponents of the idea of specialty hospitals argue that they could only improve the efficiency and quality of healthcare delivery, its critics contend that they would deplete community hospitals of their most lucrative and cost-offsetting patients, on who they depend to survive. This in fact could also happen, as we noted earlier, to a public system operating side by side a private system, due to the reduction in pricing at private hospitals that competitive forces, would eventually engender. The point in fact is that the need for attention to quality would be central to future of healthcare delivery, regardless of the funding model of health systems, and healthcare ICT has a major role to play in improving the quality of healthcare delivery. In addition, and in doing so, these technologies help reduce healthcare costs, hence health spending, enabling the achievement of the dual healthcare delivery objectives mentioned earlier. Surgical waiting lists in Regina and Saskatoon, for examples have 1,600 fewer names on them, as the 2006 annual report by the Saskatchewan Health Department showed, the result of collaborative efforts, in which healthcare ICT played a key role in the efficient information sharing and communication crucial to achieving this result. It is undeniable that the province is not only providing its residents improved health services, but also would be reducing morbidity- related health spending, in other words, achieving the dual healthcare delivery goals, which the more its doctors embrace healthcare ICT therefore, it is reasonable to assume, it would even more. Contemporary and future healthcare delivery would lean heavily on these technologies to delivery the promise to the peoples in a new era by their health systems, the need for these health systems to promote their adoption by their doctors therefore, no longer optional.

References

1. Kohn, LT., Corrigan, JM., and Donaldson, MS. To Err is Human. Building a Safer Health System. IOM Publication, National Academy Press, Washington,
D.C. (1999)

2. Institute of Medicine. Crossing the Quality Chasm: A New Health System for the 21st Century. Washington, DC: National Academy Press, 2001.

3. Brennan, Troyen A.; Leape, Lucian L.; Laird, Nan M., et al. Incidence of adverse events and negligence in hospitalized patients: Results of the Harvard Medical Practice Study I. N Engl J Med. 324:370 376, 1991.

4. Leape, Lucian L.; Brennan, Troyen A.; Laird, Nan M., et al. The Nature of Adverse Events in Hospitalized Patients: Results of the Harvard Medical Practice Study II. N Engl J Med. 324(6):377 384, 1991.

5. Thomas, Eric J.; Studdert, David M.; Burstin, Helen R., et al. Incidence and Types of Adverse Events and Negligent Care in Utah and Colorado. Med Care
forthcoming Spring 2000.

6. Thomas, Eric J.; Studdert, David M.; Newhouse, Joseph P., et al. Costs of Medical Injuries in Utah and Colorado. Inquiry. 36:255 264, 1999.

7. Johnson, W.G.; Brennan, Troyen A.; Newhouse, Joseph P., et al. The Economic Consequences of Medical Injuries. JAMA. 267:2487 2492, 1992.

8. Available at:
http://www.cbc.ca/story/world/national/2005/11/03/commonwealth-health051103.html
Accessed on September 7, 2006

9. Preventing Medication Errors. Committee on Identifying and Preventing Medication Errors. Board on Healthcare Services. IOM National Academy Press, Washington, D.C. (2006)

10. Available at:
http://www.medicalnewstoday.com/medicalnews.php?newsid=51358&nfid=al Accessed on September 10, 2006

11. Johnston, V. R., J. Hummel, T. Kinnerger, et al. Immediate Steps towards Patient Safety . Healthcare Financial Management 58, no. 2 (February 2004): 56 61.

12. Dixon, J. F. Going Paperless with Custom -Built Web-based Patient Occurrence Reporting. Joint Commission Journal on Quality Improvement 28, no. 7 (2002): 387 95.

13. Atheron, T. Description and Outcomes of the Doctor Quality Incident Reporting System Used at Baylor Medical Center at Grapevine. Baylor University Medical Center Proceedings 15 (2002): 203 8.

14. Kaushal, R., K. N. Barker, and D. W. Bates. How Can Information Technology Improve Patient Safety and Reduce Medication Errors in Children s Health Care? Archives of Pediatrics and Adolescent Medicine 155 (2001): 1002 7.

15. Bates, D. W., S. Evans, H. Murff, et al. Detecting Adverse Events Using Information Technology . Journal of the American Medical Informatics Association 10, no. 2 (2003): 115 28.

16. Available at: http://www.ihealthbeat.org/index.cfm?action=dspItem&itemID=116367&change dID=109827 Accessed on September 9, 2006

17. Available at: http://www.healthcareitnews.com/story.cms?id=5282 Accessed on September 9, 2006

18. Available at: http://www.bcma.org/public/news_publications/publications/policy_papers/ITPa per/Getting%20IT%20Right.pdf Accessed on September 09, 2006

19. Available at: http://content.healthaffairs.org/cgi/content/abstract/hlthaff.25.w412 Accessed on September 10, 2006

20. Available at: http://www.healthcareitnews.com/story.cms?id=5298 Accessed on September 10, 2006

21. Available at: http://www.healthcareitnews.com/printStory.cms?id=5471 Accessed on September 10, 2006

22. Available at: http://www.healthcareitnews.com/story.cms?id=5473 Accessed on September 10, 2006

23. Available at: http://www.itbusiness.ca/it/client/en/home/News.asp?id=40514&cid=2 Accessed on September 11, 2006

24. Available at: http://www.itbusiness.ca/it/client/en/home/News.asp?id=40514&cid=2 Accessed on September 11, 2006

25. Sheps S. Governance for patient safety: lessons from the non-health risk- critical high-reliability industries. Ottawa: Health Canada; 2005.

26. Kondro W. Independent federal safety board needed to prevent adverse events. CMAJ 2006; 174(12):1699-700.

27. Available at: http://www.itworldcanada.com/a/Daily-News/43a688ec-da8e- 40bf-81b4-bd98db346fd3.html Accessed on September 12, 2006

28. Available at: http://news.com.com/2102-7344_3-6114031.html?tag=st.util.print Accessed on September 12, 2006

Emerging Healthcare Information and Communication Technologies

Many continue to raise questions regarding the face validity of healthcare information and communication technologies, and to seek tangible evidence of their benefits to healthcare delivery1, 2. Dr Jaan Sidorov, for example, an associate in the department of general internal m edicine at Geisinger Medical Center in Danville, Pa. in a paper published in the July/August 2006 issue of Health Affairs, questioned the benefits of electronic health records (EHRs) in ambulatory care1. A recent report by U.K-based independent think-thank, the Institute for Public Policy Research (IPPR) lamented the chances of defective planning/evaluation and of lack of evidence on the benefits of the technologies, jeopardizing the public and political support for spending on ICT investments in health services2. Specifically, the IPPR report also noted such flaws in the National Health Service (NHS) s pilot services, for examples, electronic patient records trials that did not confirm the potential for improved service flexibility, care quality, or cost savings or of electronic appointment booking systems that for patients choice on treatment render estimates of benefits just hypothetical.

Furthermore, the task of justifying to doctors and other healthcare professionals, and indeed, all healthcare stakeholders, the value of investing in these technologies, crucial to their widespread diffusion for health services delivery, would be Herculean, given these circumstances. The U.K has embarked on a number of healthcare ICT pilot projects, for examples, the Interactive Digital Television (iDTV) pilot projects, Electronic Transmission of Prescriptions (ETP) Pilot Project, the National Booking Programme, the Electronic Systems Implementation Project, the National electronic Library for Health (NeLH), the Electronic Record Development and Implementation Programme (ERDIP), and the NHS Direct Online. IPPR considered the evaluation of these and other projects essential and should link expressly to the projects stated objectives, with sufficient time and resources allotted to the appraisals, and the relevant data/information gathered to facilitate project-value evaluation. No doubt, several studies have demonstrated the benefits of healthcare ICT in improving the quality of healthcare delivery, but also in simultaneously reducing health spending, for example, a recent Rand Corp. that showed that national adoption of the EHRs in the U.S. could lead to over $81 billion in annual savings3. It is also doubtless, nonetheless, that these recommendations are important. Appraising the U.K pilot and other healthcare ICT projects for example, would likely reveal some of the reasons that they are not delivering on their promises, creating opportunities for rectifying the problems involved. Regarding the Sodorov study, the author confirmed the potential value of EHRs in facilitating pay-for- performance (P4P) programs and managing chronically ill patients, and that these technologies constitute one of the tools for improving healthcare delivery. Again, it is important to consider the issues brought up in the study to understand the obstacles that might be in the way of healthcare ICT delivering their full potential. In this context, some experts concurred that his findings might reflect the fact that many EMR/EHR end -users have not installed some of the technologies advanced features, hence reducing the chances of deriving maximum benefits from the technologies, namely the realization of the dual healthcare delivery goals mentioned earlier. In other words, healthcare ICT is indeed beneficial to healthcare delivery, but we need to pay attention to a variety of issues capable of derailing our efforts to exploit their potential value. One key such issue is performance appraisal, which would for example enable improvements to some current electronic medical records (EMR) technologies that doctors claim compromise rather than enhance productivity, problems that might require developing products with less steep learning curves, or more user- friendly graphical user interface (GUI), or even upgrad es to their functionalities, for examples. In fact, the inherent desirability of continuous improvement in the quality and versatility of these technologies, coupled with the equally fluid milieu in which they are operational considering what some would consider the frenetic pace of progress in medical knowledge, for example, makes the pursuit of the delivery of the highest care quality at once elusive, yet imperative. It also underscores the need for us to continually decompose the issues involved in the delivery of health services, with a view to exposing the underlying issues and processes, even those cryptic, addressing which utilizing the appropriate healthcare ICT, which technologies the exercise would reveal, would move us progressively, and positively, along the quality spectrum. Furthermore, and in a cascading dyadic, the intercourse of medical and technological progress would likely result in the emergence of healthcare information and communication technologies that would be even more efficient and effective in moving healthcare delivery along this path. To accentuate the importance of performance evaluation on this process, the U.S. Health and Human Services Secretary Michael Leavitt recently called on a federal panel to establish the best way to measure patient-care quality, precisely and electronically4, the Secretary emphasizing the dearth of appropriate measures of the quality of patient care, the interest in the exercise however, robust. Speaking further in an address in August 2006 at the American Health Information Community (AHIC) meeting, Leavitt noted, We re all talking a good game, but we don t have the capacity to actually measure quality . There were also calls for providing more electronic support for increasingly used quality measures, including for example developing technical specifications for the quality/ performance measures for hospital and ambulatory care that the National Committee on Quality Assurance (NCQA) developed, essentially for stipulating technical standards to which vendors developing reporting solutions must adhere. As we noted earlier, continuous quality appraisals would engender the creativity that drives the emergence of novel technologies, among others, which would ultimately improve the quality of care and reduce health spending, hence the need for us to not just encourage but also spearhead the appraisals. The variety of healthcare ICT that emerges from these and other process analyses of health and healthcare delivery, encompassing the decomposition/exposition exercise mentioned earlier is testimony to the value of the exercises, if not indeed, to their pivotal role in our achieving the dual healthcare delivery objectives on an enduring basis. Consider the linkage of genetic testing for example to electronic medical records (EMR) technologies, and its potential implications for healthcare delivery, for example in primary disease prevention, and beyond, technology that would also for example, beside enabling the completion of on-site genetic testing facilitate the integration of the data with legacy information systems by healthcare facilities. The outcome of collaboration between Cerner Corp, Protedyne, and Correlagen Diagnostics, Inc, this novel technology would obviate the need for hospitals and clinics to outsource genetic testing, thereby, among others, saving significant costs5. The technology comprises GeneExplorer genetic testing software and Radius robot, by Correlagen and Protodyne, respectively, and Cerner s Millenium PathNet Helix software, the integrator with the clinic/ hospital s EHR. Radius robot, a scaled down version of the original industrial robot, is also low - priced, and with Correlagen s software offer testing for different diseases, drug responses, gene types, and to a variety of medical specialties, and both with Cerner s software, make patient s genetic results available via the EHR, at the point of care (POC.) According to Peter Massaro, chief technical officer at Protodyne, this blend of all technologies facilitates the geneticist s work by speeding up the analytical process, adding If there is a sick patient with a strange genetic disease, the hospital can provide test results in three or four days instead of three or four months. Consider also likely value to healthcare delivery of new technologies with potential solutions to the identity management problems hindering the widespread deployment of healthcare ICT such as Windows Cardspace, previously termed, InfoCard, technologies that would no doubt gain increasing currency in the near future in the health sector. CardSpace is a part of the Microsoft .NET Framework version 3.0, previously termed WinFX, the technology aimed as simplifying yet securing using digital identities, and replacing username/password as identity verifiers on the Internet. Should Microsoft, which already promised that its Window Vista new identity management technology would remove obstacles to enterprise access management, enabling persons in an organization to allow outsiders system access independent of its IT unit, not consider customizing these technologies for use in the health sector, considering both the potential massive vertical and horizontal market opportunities this could create? Would entrusting secure access control to resource owners, the main role of information cards in any enterprise, medical or otherwise not further empower the end -user, while not compromising information security, hence encourage user buy-in, the lack of which hinders the adoption of healthcare ICT in many healthcare organizations? Would these technologies not also promote the healthcare ICT adoption by the public for example that of personal health records (PHR) by reducing the policy hurdles often involved in permitting a third party access to corporate resources? With CardSpace, for example enabling access by specific outsiders via their PHRs for example, to particular information resources at say a hospital by its custodians on conducting their own risk evaluation, would it not be fostering bidirectional patient/doctor information exchange? Would the effective deployment of identity protocols/technologies, of which others such as iNames and OpenID, are also on the market, not enhance trust by all users in healthcare ICT, and help promote its diffusion among healthcare stakeholders?

The Internet has proven to be an invaluable resource to healthcare delivery. Its potential value in the health sector, however, is immense, with self-evolving networks and autonomic communications, among other novel concepts evolving on the Internet technologies of the future. Many Web-based resources currently exist for both healthcare professionals and the public on a variety of health issues. However, in many cases, as resources for doctors and other healthcare professionals, they are still isolated databases the need for connecting which to other knowledge forms in meaningful ways is dire, for example, biomarker phenotypes and associated pathways, and could, in this specific instance, improve significantly the benefits derivable from these databases on drug toxicity. To decipher the cause of drug toxicity from secondary, nontoxic drug effects, or what effects seen in vitro are applicable in vivo, and indeed, from animal to human, for examples, would require more than compiling lists of biomarker signatures to drug toxicity effects. The need for integrating all forms of data, information, and knowledge intelligently and for manifold uses across application and organizational borders is driving interests in the Semantic Web s data semantic approaches. The Sem antic Web, at whose vanguard is the World Wide Web Consortium (W3C) at MIT, whose leader, Sir Tim Berners-Lee, invented the World Wide Web around 1990, working at CERN, would simplify direct access to knowledge, internal/external to an enterprise, not only adding knowledge important for but also accelerating, decision making the physical knowledge source or its form, irrelevant. By enabling linkages between disparate internal/external databases and facilitating new knowledge capture, and by being a veritable pathway modeling and analysis instrument, the Semantic Web would ease the derivation of more-valuable information and better predictability from available data that could be crucial to patient management, and the delivery of cost-effective, and qualitative health services. The health industry produces massive information on an ongoing basis, and continues to struggle with integrating data and information from its many disparate databases, many having tried, any of the numerous approaches available such as distributed object-oriented data models, remote procedure calls, or Java-based Web tools to no avail. Experts affirm that Semantic Web technologies, which simply put converts Web data currently designed for only human readability into a machine-readable format that a computer could aggregate into types and query and from which it could infer associations, would change all that, the applications of these technologies in medicine, public health, clinical trials, and research, among others, potentially huge. Indeed, experts, many who consider the Semantic Web as the next chapter of the World Wide Web (WWW) predict the widespread adoption of these technologies, including in the health sector in the next three to five years. W3C is also keen on the security aspect of the Semantic Web, holding a workshop on Languages for privacy policy negotiation and semantics-driven enforcement , in Ispra, Italy in mid -October 2006. The workshop, aimed at IT-industry and privacy researchers worldwide tackling issues emanating from the increased rates of digital exchange of personal information, a subject of particular relevance to the health sector, for example the need to integrate technologies utilized for privacy control with varied systems and milieus, is no doubt pertinent to developments in Web technologies. Thus, the need to address privacy and information security issues in these milieus, including legacy systems and advanced emerging technologies for examples cross-business processes, service-oriented architectures, novel web applications, and web services, is paramount, not least in the health industry where they are gaining currency, and where such issues left unattended to, could compromise progress in their widespread deployment7. With the Semantic web, the doctor say that needs data from five websites would no longer need to visit each to for example cut and paste the data to obtain a unitary picture. It is possible to configure a Semantic web browser to visit numerous websites, identify, retrieve, and display in it, the required data/information, essentially to migrate data assemblage from the desktop into the network. There could be no gainsaying the potential value of such a browser in providing doctors crucial information at the point of care (POC.) With W3C developing standards for, data description and identification, the Resource Description Framework (RDF), among others, used by Semantic Web along with current data formatting and tagging standards for examples, XML, which would no doubt facilitate access to data in different web sites, the diffusion of these technologies including in the health industry is likely to proceed rapidly thenceforth. Interestingly, at the recent the Carson Future of Web Apps conference held in Mid -September 2006 in San Francisco, Adobe demonstrated the TagTV. Its agent dragged images from YouTube and Flickr, and placed them on a Web-based desktop, but also was able to drag the TagTV application off the Web page, and running it on the PC desktop, essentially freeing it from the browser, which no doubt also has potential applications in the health sector. Healthcare organizations are showing interest, increasingly in these and other novel web-based technologies, for example, the University of North Carolina Health Care System plan to license IBM s technology to create a Web-based system to replace its paper-based system. The new system termed, WebClinical Information Systems (WebCIS), comprising unified medical records that IBM recently announced, would provide access to medical data/information on a million patients via a secure Web site8. The healthcare organization will u tilize IBM s Health Information Framework that taps on open standards in the health industry, coalescing patient data/information from disparate sources, for examples, the GP s office, pharmacy, the labs, and others, and making them available to doctors and other healthcare providers rapidly, at the point of care (POC.) An ER doctor for example, would be able to view full patient information, for example on drugs, allergies, previous lab results and X- rays, and previous treatments. That developments in Internet technologies as with those described above would play an important role in healthcare delivery in the near future, is not in doubt, and one of the keys to the success of these technologies in this regard is the speed with which data and information travel across the Internet. This is clearly an important consideration in healthcare delivery where seconds could make the difference between life and death, an assurance of the speed of internet connection, hence indeed its performance in this regard, no longer the exclusive preserve of the Internet Service Provider, with which, many healthcare organizations deal. Researchers of the IST- sponsored MOME project concluded on 31 March 2006 built the knowledge and resources for such internet performance appraisal9. The goal of MOME was to build a publicly accessible data repository on the tools and data utilized for internet performance evaluation, its accessible online public database of IP (Internet Protocol) performance-measurement tools and data, essentially an online catalogue. There one could find the tool needed for a specific purpose, such as to examine denial of service attacks, as project coordinator Felix Strohmeier of Salzburg Research in Austria, noted . The IP measurement tools database has information on both open-source and commercially available tools and programs, and indeed a few that did not reveal the source code, or is otherwise unspecified. While MOME pioneered this research area in Europe, CAIDA research association at the San Diego Supercomputing Center in California, conducted research on IP measurement for almost a decade, and has released its own database of measurement tools, too to the public, the result of collaboration with MOME. Related research projects, for example the project 6QM, also IST-sponsored, aims to develop measurement technologies for Quality of Service in IPv6 networks, the researchers creating an all-inclusive system that integrate the variety of functions necessary for QoS measurement, for examples, packet capturing, data collection, and QoS metrics derivation, among others9. They also built a knowledge base and guidelines useful to operators and ISPs in meeting client goals in IPv6 advanced QoS services assuredly. There is no doubt about the importance of these seemingly benign evaluations and services to the seamless operations of healthcare information systems networks. Advances in which direction therefore, would increasingly be of interest not just to IT departments of large healthcare organizations, but also to individual healthcare practitioners, in particular as these and related technologies emerge in forms that the average user could deploy without any specialized or programming knowledge or skills, as they probably eventually would. This is what, for example, the Daidalos project is all about, that is, to design advanced network interfaces for the delivery and administration of location independent, optimized personal Services10. Currently in phase 2, Daidalos is at the helm of the re-conceptualization of network backbones needed to build the user-focused communication infrastructure of the future. The project aims to integrate diverse network technologies thereby providing ISPs/network operators, opportunities for novel user-friendly service/products value propositions to their clients and the clients ease of access to and operations of a variety of personalized data/voce, and multimedia services with ease, enhancing user experience, stationary, or on the go. This technology would be invaluable in healthcare delivery in particular with the increasing numbers of health information websites and other resources on the Internet, the equally increasing complexity of technologies, for example 3G systems, and upgrades of these and other technologies, that nonetheless are gaining increasingly public acceptance, and would with time become portals for health information communication and sharing. This highlights the point regarding the increasing likelihood of health information delivery, and indeed, healthcare delivery as a whole at any of the three primary, secondary, and tertiary, prevention levels, via some of the newer concepts of the Internet, such as the so-called Web 2.0, as healthcare providers increasingly appreciate their potential for widespread information dissemination.

The value of social network in health information dissemination regarding imminent health problems, for example, the recent warning of an outbreak of E.coli infections traced to bagged spinach in the mid -September in the U.S. from which there was one reported death and several ill, is not disputable. The health sector would likely increasingly use such avenues as Web 2.0 offers for such purposes. Besides social networking, blogs and wikis, collaboration, back-office saas, ajax, mashup tools, folksonomies, and enterprise web 2.0, are emerging Internet concepts that the health sector would increasingly have to become familiar with and to embrace. This would enable them exploit the opportunities Web 2.0 tools and technologies offer for improving the quality of healthcare delivery cost-effectively, hence in achieving the dual healthcare delivery goals, mentioned earlier. Web 2.0, which experts define differently essentially concerns the idea of content being free, in order words, fostering interactive content usage among a community of persons, its tools and methods aimed at facilitating this interaction, for example ajax, for developing interactive web applications hence accelerating web pages interactivity, speed, and utility. In the case of the E.coli poisoning mentioned above, bloggers for example affected by the illness in describing their experiences, or those who only knew others it affected, the experiences of these persons, would be creating content modifiable as the illness progresses. This could help also in deterring those that might otherwise not take the warning to avoid bagged spinach seriously from consuming it, with the potential to save lives and prevent morbidities. Other web 2.0 tools have their peculiar benefits including in the health field. Folkosonomies and the accompanying tagging for example, could transform information making it easier to search, find and to explore over time besides being viewable as a shared vocabulary its users are accustomed to, making medical and related concepts easier for the community to grasp, again with the potential to change behaviors for healthier ones, hence improve health and well being. Wikis, for example, Wikipedia, another commons-based peer production system, enable possibilities for participants to modify content, the outcome of the production process, often akin in accuracy and sophistication, to that experts produced. In other words, that participants are able to modify content does not necessarily degrade it. On the contrary, it has the potential to upgrade content started with, giving clearer and more accurate descriptions of symptoms and signs of certain diseases for instance based albeit on the experiences of participants or of those known to them, and perhaps more importantly expressed in the language and manner best understandable to community members. This not only makes it easier for the health system to rectify the pervasive information asymmetry that continues to compromise healthcare delivery and the system s ability to achieve the dual healthcare delivery objectives, but also empowers the public, and encourages it to implement healthcare ICT, further enhancing the health systems prospects of achieving its goals. This issue is particularly poignant with research evidence indicating that the manner of expression of the content of a significant percentage of government health-information websites is way above the educational levels, of many persons even in countries such as the U.S. Besides, certain groups of persons, for example, the young, might just prefer to express themselves, even on health issues, in particular ways. The developments in web technologies discussed thus far are somewhat interlin ked, Web 2.0, some would argue, a prelude to the semantic web, even if the tools and approaches that constitute the former do not include an Internet with machines able to understand and ferret meaning from data and information. Furthermore, more novel and innovative concepts and tools, such as podcasts, weblogs, RSS feeds, social software, web APIs, and online web services among others increasingly fall under the Web 2.0 rubric, broadening the scope of new technologies, and methods available to the health sector for health information dissemination, among other health services, and to which use it could put them. It is instructive for healthcare providers and others in the healthcare industry the rather tight social fabric among persons that have emanated from the use of the varieties of Web 2.0 technologies and tools. This is an attribute that those specialties such as mental health and psychiatry could find useful in some form of group therapy and support to individuals that have any of a range of conditions. The interactive content modification that goes on in these communities could also inspire interest in seeking additional information on health issues from other sources, for example, the individual s GP, or alert another to the seriousness or otherwise of previous or ongoing experiences, prompting medical consultation. There are now also websites based on Ajax programming that behave pretty much like PC applications, for examples, capable of word processing, which could be useful, to healthcare professionals on the go, doctors and other such professionals able to enjoy browser-based operating system (OS) milieus wherever they are within or outside the hospital/clinic. To underscore the potential for creativity of the developments in web technologies, albeit in collaboration with others, Kochi Shimbun, IBM Japan, and PERS Japan plans to conduct a three-day field experiment. They will distribute newspaper articles to bedside terminals at hospitals, commencing September 14 200611. The beside-terminal would operate as a TV and video monitor and would offer several functions for examples access to the World Wide Web and medical diagnosis logs. IBM Japan s technology will transform digital article data into a digital paper and put on view images and text rapid ly and effortlessly on the beside-terminal, the firm even offering to provide functionalities to link a specific part of the digital paper to a video or associated website. There is no doubt that healthcare delivery could benefit immensely from the emerging technologies that we have discussed thus far, but indeed, many other promising such technologies with potential applications in the health industry including mobile monitoring applications for patients and their care providers. These technologies would be increasingly important in the efforts to achieve the dual healthcare delivery goals, in particular in the treatment of chronically ill people whose condition often requires regular monitoring, yet who often have impaired mobility, may leave too far way from healthcare facilities, or are too frail to go there. In fact, coverage and access issues in healthcare are not easing in many countries, making the need for technologies that would help in solving these problems even more urgent. In the U.S., for example, virtually all states will experience a scarcity of primary care physicians by 2020, a recent report released on September 27, 2006, by the American Academy of Family Physicians (AAFP) noted 12. According to the report, the U.S. will need 39% more primary care doctors over the next decade and a half to meet higher demand, due in the main to popu lation growth and an aging population particularly in states such as Arizona, Florida, Nevada, Texas and Idaho. That only half as many doctors opting to specialize in primary compared to other specialties perceived as more lucrative between 1997 and 2005, reveals the potential severity of this trend. This, viewed in the context of the key role of primary care doctors, the first doctors most people see when they are ill, essentially initiating the rest of the consultation and care process, and of the increasing need for these doctors in an aging population, underscores the need to encourage doctors to specialize in primary care medicine. It would also help to reform medical liability law s, and to review their reimbursement system with a view to increasing their pay, certainly not to follow through with the proposed 5.1% scheduled reduction in Medicare physician reimbursements scheduled for 2007. This issue also underscores the need to promote the widespread use of healthcare ICT, key to integrating the fragmented health system responsible for the disjointed and complicated service provision that partly undermines primary care, and makes the specialty unattractive to doctors planning to specialize. Indeed, as AAFP President Larry Fields noted, the anticipated shortage of primary care doctors likely will prompt some to limit new patient intake, with patients then having to travel farther to find doctors or finding none at all. There is no doubt that under these circumstances, healthcare ICT, appropriately deployed, for example, in telehealth services, would be an important aspect of the solutions we seek. The issue of not just scarcity of primary care physicians, which incidentally is not a problem only in the U.S., but of the shortage of doctors in general, and of their misdistribution is one that requires thorough process cycle analyses. In other words, each health jurisdiction decomposing the relevant issues to reveal salient and fundamental sub-issues and processes peculiar to the health jurisdiction that the implementation of the appropriate healthcare ICT could help resolve, and what these technologies are.

Regardless of the issues a particular health jurisdiction faces, doctors would need to adopt these technologies for the health system to derive any benefits from them. This is considering the central role of doctors in healthcare delivery, hence would need whatever encouragement they could receive in so doing, for example, the pilot grants by Massachusetts to doctors for electronic medical records (EMR) systems. In Canada, the government in Alberta is doing a similar thing providing its doctors with grants to purchase these systems, an important prelude in the overall efforts to implement electronic health records (EHR) by health jurisdictions. Similarly, we should encourage the healthcare consumer to embrace personal health records technologies, which integrated into these other two would offer bidirectional information flow, giving both patients and doctors, access to valuable information to both, billing, and health information, respectively, for examples, fostering qualitative healthcare delivery, even in disparate locations, and cost-effectively. These issues are spawning innovative technologies in a variety of healthcare information and communication technologies domains, such as in application development, security, and wired and wireless networking, in particular, wireless/mobile solutions potentially able to solve not just the problem of access to patient information at the point of care (POC,) but also those relating to ambulatory/ domiciliary patient management. Both these issues, as we noted earlier would feature quite prominently in the healthcare delivery programs of the future particularly in the developed countries with an increasingly aging population and even those not so developed ones with a similar problem. Considering that, the security of patient information and other data/information that healthcare providers would necessarily communicate and share to execute the various healthcare delivery programs would be crucial not just to their success but to whether or not they take off in the first place, technological innovation in certain areas are intense. These include cyber threats, wireless security, authentication, encryption, data/disaster recovery, intrusion detection, and firewalls. Consider for example, the announcement on September 26, 2006, by the U.S. Federal Communications Commission (FCC) that it would establish a pilot program to help public and non-profit healthcare providers set up state and regional broadband networks devoted to healthcare services, and provide the networks the funds that would enable them connect to Internet2 s countrywide advanced research and education network. The aim of the program, which FCC would revitalize the current Rural Health Care funding mechanism to kick-start, among others is to foster the establishment of an advanced healthcare network that would facilitate access by the public to first-rate healthcare services, resources, and research. According to the FCC, which has started soliciting applications from interested parties, the pilot program will fund up to 85% of the costs used in implementing state or regional broadband networks dedicated to health care13. It will also provide money for up to 85% of the costs needed to link the regional and/or statewide to Internet2 (a dedicated nationwide backbone linking a number of government research institutions) and acad emic, public, and private health care institutions, repositories of medical expertise and information. FCC plans to cap the funds at an amount not more than the difference between that devoted under the existing program for 2006 and $100 million (25% of th e annual $400 million cap on rural health care spending)13. Dr. Michael McGill, in charge of Internet2 s health sciences program, noted that the program is a significant step towards realizing the potential of advanced Internet technology to enhance the quality and availability of healthcare services by improving access to medical expertise, facilitating the flow of information for research, and streamlining care processes and costs. By linking high-speed state and regional research and education networks, the nationwide Internet2 backbone already links over 46,000 research and education institutions with high-performance, highly-reliable networking14. Would such a program not in fact also help rectify the information asymmetry pervasive in the health sector, one which hinders the ability of the healthcare consumer to make rational decisions about health and service provision issues, which no doubt compromises that of the health system to achieve the dual healthcare delivery goals of qualitative yet cost-effective health service provision? The project also exemplifies the collaborative spirit that would pervade health information-technology development in the coming years as both public and private sector organizations seek solutions to problems common to their organizations as the complex maze of contemporary health issues are wont to be. This collaboration of Internet2 members, for examples, the National Institutes of Health (NIH), plus over a hundred other linked healthcare organizations and medical schools on advanced Internet technologies that bolster health sciences has enormous potential. Examples include its influence on the multidirectional interactivity among patients, doctors, and students, including development of virtual surgery technologies for training the latter remotely by experts, worldwide, telemedicine applications that make expertise from specialist centers accessible to patients in rural areas, and identity management technologies offering privacy control and assuring the confidentiality of patients medical records. These are no doubt, benefits that move us closer toward achieving the dual healthcare delivery. They also suggest to us those derivable from such collaborative efforts, and the likely evolution of innovative healthcare information and communication technologies in the future from such enterprises, which would be essentially the wellspring of the creativity in technological bent that would in turn inspire novel healthcare delivery models, and vice versa, in a continuum of progress in both domains. Developments in broadband communications technologies are making it possible for health care providers to improve access to qualitative care, and helping to solve not just the problem of lack of access to care many in rural and remote areas even in developed countries, but also those pertaining to shortage of doctors and other healthcare professionals, and/or their misdistribution. With progress in telehealth applications, including telemedicine, for example, it would be easier, faster, and more cost-effective to provide specialists services in virtually any area of medicine for example in radiology, pediatrics, cardiology, to peoples in such areas. This would also be convenient for the elderly and frail, for examples, and the reduced hospital stays that would result, would help reduce healthcare costs. Emerging healthcare ICT would increasingly aim to address specific healthcare issues in the context of a whole, which would shift the conceptualization of healthcare software and other ICT from mere facilitators of healthcare delivery processes to actually becoming embedded in these process, assimilated, and becoming constitutive . Emerging healthcare ICT would therefore be a part of the entire effort to improve the health system and make it more efficient and cost-effective. They would emerge from the dyadic of healthcare delivery and their technologies, an essentially symbiotic wherein the outcome of process cycle analyses, that of the decomposition/exposition continuum of healthcare issues and processes, would feed into the latent or indeed, ongoing creative mechanisms in the healthcare ICT domain. This explains the need for the active participation of doctors in these processes that ultimately lead to the overall outcome, that of healthcare delivery. This is more so considering that they are the major agents for health services delivery, hence are quite conversant with the issues involved at least from the clinical perspective, which assumes that there are others, which indeed, there are, many at first seemingly at best only remotely related, but nonetheless operate in tandem, with the clinical to realize this outcome. All concerned would need to continue to work together and individually identify key research areas that would further elicit perhaps even cryptic issues germane to the evolution of healthcare delivery in its multifarious dimensions, to meet the ever-changing needs of health services, an appreciation of this flux crucial to conceptualizing healthcare delivery as perennially imperfect yet potentially so. This reinvention of our mindset regarding healthcare delivery would inspire progress in healthcare information and communication technologies on an equally fluid evolutionary path. Should the prospects of improving healthcare d elivery on a continuous, permanent basis, not inspire us to attend to these issues with all our vigor? Many countries in the developed world for example are aging, a healthy society, and active workforce crucial determinants of sustainable productivity and economic growth in these countries, recognition of the potential contribution of their human capital to economic wealth even more urgent and dire. However, this calls for nothing short of an intense devotion to such principles as those enunciated above, principles that underscore the need for people to be healthy, physically and mentally, in the first place to be productive and to accumulate and provide human capital. These principles also emphasize the need for us to view health as long-term investment in human capital and not just costs, even as we aim to achieve the dual healthcare delivery goals. As noted above, developments in healthcare ICT would influence those in healthcare delivery, and vice versa, the quest to boost these developments, for examples recent accomplishments in genomics and the increased significance of genetics in healthcare, which no doubt have had a major effect on clinical practice and research, involve determining other key areas for biomedical and medical informatics research. The integration for example of genomic and molecular medicine, is leading to more in-depth understanding of life and disease via the presence and regulation of molecular entities, and to customized healthcare delivery, the application of genotypic knowledge to identify disease proneness, hence develop treatment modalities tailored to individual patients genotypes. The promotion of such knowledge is the primary goal of many research projects worldwide for example, the IST-funded SYMBIOmatics project. The project has already noted the status of research in biomedical informatics in Europe, and thirty-one areas of future research opportunity, in a White Paper presented at the ICT for Bio- Medical Sciences conference in Brussels on 29-30 June 2006, the areas narrowed to thirteen, namely; medical genetics databases and initiatives, and gene expression information in medical diagnostics and prognostics15. Others are modeling and simulation of biological structures, processes, and diseases, integration of data from biosensors and medical devices with clinical information systems, integration of patient molecular data into electronic health records, systems for clinical decision making, semantic interoperability and ontologies in biomedicine, and technologies for biom edical information integration. The remaining areas are data interoperability and standards, connecting biobanks to large-scale databases to enable data mining, patient-risk profiling, and lifestyle management, applied pharmaceutical research, and clinical and ethical issues related to biomedical data processing. Considering the symbiotic dyadic mentioned earlier between healthcare delivery and healthcare information and communication technologies, these identified priority research areas would likely spawn novel and innovative healthcare ICT in the coming years that would have profound effects on not just the practice of medicine, but also our efforts to achieve the dual healthcare delivery goals. Indeed, explaining why these areas are such high priority, Graham Cameron of the European Bioinformatics Institute (EBI-EMBL) near Cambridge, UK, said, In pharmaco- genomics for example, it is well-known that certain drugs will work well on some people, but not on others. We believe that genetic makeup is an important explanation, but genetic testing is needed to confirm that view. Continuing, he said, Research in these areas could well bring down the cost of genetic testing enough to put it within the reach of the GP practice. So that GPs would be able to test patients for suitability as to certain treatments before commencing treatment with a particular drug. You could work out, with the help of your GP, if your own cholesterol level or diet is dangerous for you personally, according to your genetic makeup. Imagine the difference this could make for personal lifestyle choices! Imagine.

There is no doubt about the significant role that healthcare information and communication technologies would play in the delivery of qualitative and cost-effective health services in the years ahead, the country in question notwithstanding. Progress is ongoing in different aspects of this domain that would influence medicine profound, and that doctors need to be aware of being key drivers in the healthcare delivery enterprise. For example, on September 26, 2006, Intel revealed an 80-core processor at its developer forum in San Francisco. A key feature of the chip is the linkage of each core directly to a 256MB memory chip via a technology called Through Silicon Vias, or TSV16 , the memory coupled to the processor cores that potentially could be all the memory a computer needs, TSV use possible in a wide range of chips, and not only the 80-core processor. Hence, computer makers, in building a system, could use the memory obtained in the processor they bought from Intel, obviating to purchase as currently, memory chips separately from other firms. Experts believe this could make the comeback of Intel, which in the 1980s, was an industry leader in the computer memory, or DRAM, market, u ntil pushed aside by Japanese competitors, although it continued to market NOR flash memory and other memory types. The use of these new chips is different from that of DRAM, the embedding of memory directly to the processor now incredibly value-added, which attests to the point made earlier about re-conceptualizing healthcare software and ICT as a whole as constitutive rather than merely facilitative, a rethinking that essentially annuls fears in some quarters regarding the commoditization of these technologies. Presently, memory and the processor in Intel-based computers exchange data via a memory controller, which is much slower than the processor, often creating holdups in computer performance, but which replaced with TSV, would no doubt speed up data shuttling. This is an attribute crucial in healthcare delivery where doctors and other healthcare providers typically need prompt and accurate data and information in real time at the point of care (POC.) Furthermore, data emerging from memory also wrings through an often-congested port, a problem that by essentially opening up thousands of ports, TSV would ease. Interestingly also, the processor cores are not limited to obtaining memory from the chip coupled as they are linked to each other via high-speed links that a router integrated into each core controls. The prototype 80-core chip has a combined memory bandwidth of 1 terabyte per second, which translates to being able to move a trillion bytes per second. In market terms, TSV would certainly put another major chipmaker, AMD, which garnered competitive edge when it released its Opteron chip, in the main from Opteron s integrated memory controller, which Intel shuns for its chips. Experts predict that while TSV might not necessarily bring Intel back into making DRAM, where making profit is quite difficult historically, it would in all likelihood, encourage Intel to market it, and in particular if DRAM operates excellently with TSV, although Intel still manufactures the not-so-cheap SRAM. Further is the technicality of devising packages that would enable the processor and memory to cohabitate, considering that the processor typically produces more heat than the memory, getting which packaging design right is crucial to the health sector reaping the benefits of this technological innovation, which would make a significant difference to healthcare delivery quality. At the same conference, Intel announced two plans to make it easier for other chipmakers to connect their own processors to the firm s17. In one, it plans to allow Xilinx and Altera, plug their special-purpose chips into its front-side bus, used currently to link its processors to others, to memory, and to all subsystems in a computer, in the other, tagged "Geneseo , co-built with IBM, it plans to perk up the commonly-used PCI (peripheral component interconnect) technology to work with disparate accelerator chips17. In its bid to outperform its competition Advanced Micro Devices (AMD), which acquired competitive edge especially in server sales in recent times, and whose technology, HyperTransport , offers direct high-speed links to and between processors, Intel continues to develop innovative technologies from which the health sector would certainly benefit. For example, Torrenza another technology built by AMD enables coprocessors for examples, graphics chips, and number crunchers, among others to plug into HyperTransport, but again, Intel is developing akin technology termed CSI, meaning Common System Interconnect/or Interface, some experts contending that PCI is more efficient regarding this functionality. Intel anticipates Geneseo would succeed PCI Express 2.0, expected out in 2007, Geneseo, expected in 2008, companies such as IBM, Dell, Hewlett-Packard, and Cisco Systems already on the list of partners signed up for Geneseo, server maker Sun Microsystems, which markets only AMD-based x86 servers, and with a strong showing in the health sector, notably absent. Several industry observers are predicting a good response to Geneseo in the accelerator market, a market closely linked with the speed and accuracy on which the success or otherwise of many of the tasks in healthcare delivery depends. Still on emerging hardware technologies relevant to healthcare delivery, also still on Intel, the firm also plans to add over four dozens novel instructions to its x86 chips, in a bid to accelerate tasks such as search, audio/video processing, and mathematical calculations. This is an instruction set extension that would doubtless benefit the health industry, and on which Microsoft and Adobe Systems are already collaborating with the firm. The new instructions, billed out in the Penryn generation of processors, in 2008, are in two categories, SSE4, fourth-generation Streaming SIMD (single instruction, multiple data) Extensions, which enables a chip operate same action with several data elements rather than require instruction pairing with each element, thereby optimizing many audio/video/graphics-related operations, and increasing efficiency, and another category. This other category accelerates two explicit applications, the first is searching and pattern-matching, invaluable in handwriting recognition, and genetic research, among others, the second, cyclical redundancy check (CRC) technology that checks data transfer integrity as it transitions between storage systems and other computers, both clearly of immense benefit in healthcare delivery. It is obvious that innovation continues apace not just in healthcare software, but also in hardware, and in many other domains for example, the Internet, broadband, and many others, all with potential benefits for our efforts to achieve the dual healthcare delivery goals. In this regard, the efforts of Intel in not just stimulating research and facilitating relevant software development, for example, announcing, actually not in keeping with its usual practice, in advance, the instruction set extension mentioned above, and promoting directly and indirectly the widespread diffusion of healthcare ICT, developing a half-size motherboard, that would be much-less priced, are commendable. The firm s half-sized motherboard, reminiscent of attempts of yore to cram in processors as densely as possible, is the S3000PT18. Code-named Port Townsend, it is about 6 inches by 13 inches, m eaning two of the motherboards can fit in a single rack-mounted machine only 1.75 inches thick, or arranged vertically, 10 in a 7-inch-thick machine. Commenting on the latter product, Dave Kennedy, a product manager at the company said, It s a poor man s blade solution , the motherboard exhibited in 10 blade servers, each blade equipped with a single four-core Xeon 3000 processor, server-inclined versions of the firm s more sophisticated Extreme line of Core 2 Duo processors. It is the more commendable that Intel is foraying into the low -end market, which faltered with the dot-com bubble burst that coincided with their market entry, besides the market being unimpressed with the processor cramming mentioned above, and with the market generally keener on second-generation models, which had more reliable higher-end blades with excellent prospects for remote management. Nonetheless, many cannot afford the high-end products and just as many could get by with low -end ones, for example, many smaller healthcare organizations, and indeed, many other organizations including in the health sector prefer to use single-processor servers at the periphery of corporate networks for tasks for examples, intrusion detection, hosting Web sites, or application servers. Indeed, in some cases, two uniprocessor servers in a rack- mount server is more efficient better than is a one dual-processor approach. Besides the S3000PT motherboards, billed on the market in October 2006 with dual-core Xeons, a quad -core version, in January 2007, Intel is actually gearing up for an age wherein it would tailor its server products to specific customer needs19. The company intends to develop a variety of combinations of processors, chipsets and design structures for future servers, deploying approach es to support different interconnect strategies or types of memory, although not necessarily jettisoning its older platforms. The firm, which is garnering strength, again in the server market since it launched its Xeon 5100 series processors still has to contend with AMD, with which its announcement of technologies such as the Common System Interconnect (CSI) mentioned earlier would no doubt help. This is because it would help Intel interlink its future multicore processors directly, and will have an integrated memory controller design such as boosted AMD s Opteron processor. Intel would likely market in future new categories of processors and chipsets for particular designs, for examples compact blade servers. It has, in fact adopted for its server processors in 2006, the FB-DIMM, or fully buffered memory, standard that permits more memory modules on servers, although the modules guzzle more power than the DDR (double data rate) memory older servers, and those by AMD do. As part of what the company termed its hyper-segmentation approach, it would likely in future also support both memory technologies for multiple server types, and develop products that use integrated memory controllers for faster processor/memory connection. It would likely develop chips with its present front-side bus design, where signals reach memory via a bus, a segmentation whose resulting product customization would fit well into the needs and workloads of specific enterprises, including healthcare organizations. This would no doubt, in particular with the prospects of pricing being equally differential make these products affordable to many smaller healthcare organizations, facilitating the widespread diffusion of healthcare ICT, and ultimately, the achievement of the healthcare delivery objectives mentioned earlier. The example of Intel, which explains our focus on it, shows the potential to marry corporate strategies with collaboration with other healthcare stakeholders in the efforts by all to achieve these dual healthcare delivery goals. In other words, not only doctors and others in the healthcare delivery fields, but also private firms, technology-based and otherwise, and government agencies, and indeed all healthcare stakeholders have a stake in achieving these dual goals. Further, their efforts toward this goal do not have to conflict with their other interests, but in fact, would complement them in the big picture, literally.

As noted earlier, there are emerging technologies and ideas in a variety of healthcare ICT domains relevant to healthcare delivery, including what some would consider esoteric ones such robotics, proteonomics, genomics, even nano- technology, these areas indeed too numerous to mention here, but some have been quite controversial, for example, mobile Internet concept and technologies. The idea being able to surf the Internet from one s handsets, for example, a cellular phone, as readily as one does on the PC at home is no doubt attractive, and has important applications in healthcare delivery, even if only for healthcare consumers to find and access health information on the go. No doubt, some mobile Internet access is already possible, with millions of people worldwide accessing wireless application protocol, or WAP, Web sites, web sites with minimal features d esigned in particular for mobile handsets, the same reasons some dismiss such sites as too restricted. Not even the suggestion by some for a new domain name, dotmobi , for Web sites optimized for mobile surfing helps appease critics, or for that matter, other suggestions such as utilizing intelligent browsers make customary Web sites viewable on small handsets20. The largestU.S. mobile carriers, Cingular Wireless, Verizon Wireless, Sprint Nextel, and T-Mobile, are already experiencing increased data usage, in the first half of 2006 generating over $6.3 billion in wireless data revenues, which in total, plus those of several regional carriers, were over $7 billion during that same period. Experts estimates of potential revenues by mobile carriers in the U.S. were over $15 billion in the entire year, an almost 75% increase over the previous year of $8.6 billion20. Consumer messaging services for examples short-message service (SMS), and enterprise data services, have made up most of these revenues in the U.S., versus mobile Internet usage by wireless customers in Japan or South Korea, where surfing the mobile Web is ubiquitous, most U.S., not so doing because they consider the features undeveloped in navigation and quality terms. This is true, and due partly to technologies web site designers and Telco s in the U.S., use, and partly because most consumers lack access to speedier 3G networks and reasonably priced 3G handsets, which no doubt significantly buoy quality. Much effort is going into improving the quality of the mobile Internet, in particular by the so-called mobile virtual network operators (MVNOs), for examples, Mobile ESPN and Helio, which offer specialized services, downloadable sports news and others sports-related services, and for young hipsters, offering them interactive games and other services, respectively. The latter has also teamed up with the MySpace social-networking Web site, offering users the ability to read and write blogs, and MySpace mail, among others, from their cellular phones. Both however, leased capacity from Sprint Nextel and do not own their own networks, hence services depend on the network speed, which is still reportedly quite slow for the download, and other services these duo offer. The newer version of the protocol, WAP 2.0, is here, and is apparently faster, the number of WAP Web sites increasing dramatically in recent years, as are those of users, which would likely increase even further as carriers deploy 3G-based, faster wireless networks and handset manufacturers market increasingly suave handsets with more processing power, memory and bigger screens. Mobile Web browsers such as Opera Mini, a free downloadable browser client made for Java-enabled cell phones would increase in numbers obviating the need to have a smart phone, for which mobile browsers often seem made, to browse on the go, and indeed, T-Mobile, is preinstalling Opera Mini into its phones. Besides new applications and browsers, users also need access to fast 3G wireless networks and 3G handsets, to have better mobile Internet experience, only roughly 7 million subscribers in the U.S., use 3G services of over 200 million, a situation not too different in the U.K. There a recent survey showed that in spite of investment by operators in services such as i-mode and Vodafone Live, 73% of respondents do not use mobile Internet, slow page-loading (38%), and hard navigation (27%) some of the reasons why21. The survey also showed that surfing habits varied based on access portal to the Internet, some happy to browse using a PC than mobile Internet, when seeking a specific piece of information, more preferring access to maps than read news and sports via their phones, 49% and 47%, respectively. This seeming disinterest in mobile has some worrying about the need to establish the firm, Mobile Top Level Domain (mTLD,) funded by a consortium of companies including Ericsson, Google, Microsoft, Nokia, Samsung Electronics, T-Mobile and Vodafone, put in charge by the Internet Corporation of Assigned Names and Numbers (ICANN) in the summer of 2005, to allocate the domain names. Nonetheless, there is no doubt about the value of mobile Internet in various aspects of healthcare delivery, although many contend that not even the top -level domain, which went live on September 26, 2006 aimed at assisting mobile surfers find sites which would display excellently on handheld devices with small screens, would solve the usual problems plaguing this technology23. Not everyone agrees that creating a dot-mobi version of a site is the panacea for these problems, many suggesting the need for web designers to recognize the potential attempts at accessing their content from a variety of portals that the increasing convergence of fixed and mobile devices engender, an important lesson for those creating such websites in the health sector. Some web sites, for example, Google, which automatically scales itself for mobile services, have imbibed this lesson, critics of dotmobi pointing out that one does not need a new domain to do that. Would it not be even quicker for drug withdrawals warnings to reach healthcare consumers via their cell phones, on the go, with the potential to save lives, were the issues regarding mobile Internet resolved than it would the new approach to web-based drug withdrawal warnings the University of Cincinnati (UC) recently developed, accessed via the PC at home? UC announced this new approach in September 2006, one that is very valuable for informing consumers online when the Food and Drug Administration (FDA) withdraws a medication24. This new method works with NetWellness.org, a commercial-free, consumer health Web site produced by UC, Case Western Reserve University, and Ohio State University, Ohio s three medical research universities. There is no doubt about the benefits to patients of this service, and as noted Peter Embi, MD, lead author on the UC-based study published recently in the Journal of Medical Internet Research, Information about drug withdrawals may not reach patients quickly enough to prevent potentially dangerous side effects. He added, Given the public s growing use of the Web for health information, it s important that Web- based consumer health content is kept up to date, particularly that involving withdrawal of a potentially harmful medicine. He added th at .. It s been shown that many sites don t update their content for days, or even weeks, following an FDA drug withdrawal, and that the new approach allows just one person to modify affected Web pages in less than an hour and within just hours of an FDA drug withdrawal announcement. This new approach no doubt has the potential to save lives as, according to Embi, There s evidence that patients continue to use medications for some time after their withdrawal, which occasionally causes harmful effects so it's important to inform the public as quickly as possible . This new approach resulted from a team effort based on the experience of Embi and his team evaluating NetWellness previous update process after the withdrawal by FDA approval for Vioxx (rofecoxib), an anti- inflammatory drug and painkiller, on Sept. 30, 2004, which took almost three weeks!! After implementing the new method, it took only 18 hours after the FDA withdrawal of the anti-inflammatory drug Bextra (valdecoxib) on April 7, 2005 to update everything about the drug on NetWellness. Indeed, this new approach, initiated by the FDA s automated MedWatch E-List alert and in conjunction with modified technology and people processes, enables updates of all relevant NetWellness pages with little or no manual input within 24 hours of FDA drug recall, which reaches the NetWellness team via an alert by

MedWatch E-List. The team instantly checks the Web site s database for all entries of the drug s name, including trade and generic names, which it then hyperlinked via an automated find-and-replace function inbuilt with the Web site s content management system. Pages referenced receive a hyperlinked warning box simultaneously to show presence of critical information on the drug, all hyperlinks pointing straight to a new NetWellness warning page. This page has information on the FDA alert and to extra links to either, the FDA or the drug maker s Web site. Incidentally a recent Journal of the American Medical Informatics Association study showed that most Web-based sources, even the popular ones, took several days to update the Bextra drug information, one such popular web site, as many as 268 days to do so24. Do these not highlight the value of such novel approaches as Embi and his team developed, and wou ld it not even been more effective, as noted earlier, for the healthcare consumer to access this Web site on the go? Would it not be necessary also to encourage the adoption of such new approaches by all Web sites purporting to provide the healthcare consu mer with current and accurate health information when in reality they are not? How could we expect to achieve the dual healthcare delivery objectives if we could not even provide the healthcare consumer with up -to-date health information, in particular on drugs that the FDA withdrew from the market, the continuing use of which might be detrimental to the user s health? Besides increasing morbidities, and perhaps even mortalities, thereby increasing health spending, do we not have a moral obligation to ensure that the health consumer receives such crucial information promptly? The answers to these questions are doubtless obvious, the issues involved further underlining the important role that healthcare information and communication technologies have to play in contemporary healthcare delivery. They also by extension highlight the need for doctors and other healthcare professionals, as Dr Embi and his team have done, for example, to lead the way with initiatives in promoting the widespread diffusion of these technologies. Such initiatives would be contributing to the achievement of the healthcare delivery goals strengthening the dyadic with the healthcare ICT domain that results in the imperative symbiosis that moves us inevitably toward these goals.

References

1. Available at: http://www.healthcareitnews.com/story.cms?id=5298 Accessed on September 14, 2006

2. Available at:

http://www.iitelecom.com/index.php?id=41&view=single&event_id=80&L= Accessed on September 14, 2006

3. Available at: http://www.rand.org/news/press.05/09.14.html Accessed on September 14, 2006

4. Available at: http://www.healthcareitnews.com/story.cms?id=5457 Accessed on September 14, 2006

5. Available at: http://www.healthcareitnews.com/printStory.cms?id=5378 Accessed on September 16, 2006

6. Available at: http://news.com.com/2102-7355_3-6115527.html?tag=st.util.print Accessed on September 16, 2006

7. Available at: http://www.w3.org/2006/07/privacy-ws/cfp.html Accessed on September 17, 2006

8. Available at:

http://news.com.com/UNC+Healthcare+to+license+IBM+technology/2110-1011_3-

6079199.html Accessed on September 17, 2006

9. Available at: http://www.6qm.org/ Accessed on September 17, 2006

10. Available at: http://www.ist-daidalos.org/default.htm Accessed on September 17, 2006

11. Available at:

http://www.medicalnewstoday.com/medicalnews.php?newsid=52033&nfid=al Accessed on September 17, 2006

12. Available at:

http://www.kaisernetwork.org/daily_reports/rep_index.cfm?DR_ID=40078 Accessed on September 27, 2006

13. Available at: http://www.fcc.gov/ Accessed on September 27, 2006

14. Available at:

http://www.himss.org/ASP/ContentRedirector.asp?ContentID=66115 Access on September 27, 2006

15. Available at:

http://istresults.cordis.lu/popup.cfm?section=news&tpl=article&ID=82832&Auto Print=True Accessed on September 28, 2006

16. Available at: http://news.com.com/2102-1006_3-6120547.html?tag=st.util.print

Accessed on September 28, 2006

17. Available at: http://news.com.com/2102-1006_3-6120237.html?tag=st.util.print Accessed on September 28, 2006

18. Available at: http://news.com.com/Intel+shows+pint- size+server+motherboard/ 2100-1010_3-6120352.html?tag=html.alert Accessed on September 28, 2006

19. Available at: http://news.com.com/2102-1010_3-6120505.html?tag=st.util.print Accessed on September 28, 2006

20. Available at: http://news.com.com/2102-1039_3-6110100.html?tag=st.util.print Accessed on September 28, 2006

21. Available at:

http://www.theregister.co.uk/2006/08/08/mobile_internet_survey/ Accessed on September 28, 2006

22. Available at: http://news.com.com/Dot- mobi+domain+for+mobile+devices+hits+the+Web/2100-1039_3-6075779.html?tag=st.rn Accessed on September 28, 2006

23. Available at: http://news.com.com/Analysts+question+the+point+of+dot- mobi/
2100-1039_3-6120263.html?tag=html.alert
Accessed on September 28, 2006

24. Available at:

http://www.medicalnewstoday.com/medicalnews.php?newsid=52738&nfid=al Accessed on September 28,
2006

ICT and Progress in Healthcare Delivery

Many developed countries have an increasingly aging population, the prevalence of chronic illnesses rising concomitantly. Such countries would likely find deploying wireless and mobile technologies more in keeping with their efforts to meet their peoples healthcare needs, cost-effectively in the years ahead. Researchers are developing novel technologies to meet the healthcare delivery challenges that these chronic illnesses and others would increasingly pose. An example of these efforts is th e HEALTHSERVICE 24 (HS24) project, which the European Commission s eTEN program funds, an inventive mobile healthcare system, which supports the mobility of both patients and health professionals, increases patients quality of life (QOL), and curtails healthcare spending. According to project coordinator Jennie Weingartner of Ericsson Germany in Düsseldorf, Our concept targets non-critical patients who use a lot of hospital resources, but because they are non-critical could be easily monitored from home H S24 gives them more freedom, while fulfilling one of Europe s e-health priorities to provide restructured, citizen-centred health systems. The system enables doctors and other healthcare professionals to provide their patients remote, qualitative follow -up treatment whenever, and wherever, the patients able to carry on with their daily routines, uninterrupted, to monitor their own physical state, and to receive information and recommendations. With the number of persons with chronic illness in Europe over the next ten years billed to increase to over 100 million, it is hard not to see the potential of mobile health services in facilitating the realization of the dual healthcare delivery goals. To illustrate the point, it costs For example, it costs about 41,000 euros for conventional treatment in the UK yearly of an individual participating in a SEDS (Supervised Exercise, Diet and Stress management) program, versus only 15,000 euros annually for mobile patient management, without compromising the quality of service delivery. Based on sophisticated concepts and technologies for examples, Body Area Networks (BAN), 2.5/3G wirelessbroadband communications (GPRS/UMTS), and wearable medical devices, persons using the HS24 platform have sensors interlinked under a BAN, managed via a PDA or cell phone, data gathered transmitted on a continuous basis via a wireless UMTS or GPRS service to the doctor or clinic. The system s content-management capabilities enable instant analysis of the individual s bio-data and personalized feedback to the person in real time via alarms/reminders, vital signs monitored including temperature, ECG, oxygen saturation, respiration, and electromyography (EMG), among others. The system makes it possible to diagnose and treat the person remotely, and for the data center to dispatch an SMS alarm or offer first-level medical support were his/her condition to deteriorate rapidly.

A cross-section of healthcare stakeholders benefit from the system, a certified commercial version of which Ericsson has developed, patients, in improved accessibility, doctors, and other healthcare professionals in enhanced efficiency and accuracy in patient follow -ups, with patient information available and accessible in real time, and patients families, in fewer hospital visits, hence transportation costs. The health system benefits from optimization of resource utilization via reduced bed occupancy for patients requiring monitoring, hence bed for the more critically ill, with costs saving in the long term, including for insurance firms, and for healthcare payers via reduced treatment costs, improved resource management, and noteworthy health-economic progress. Noted Weingartner regarding multi-site project trials conducted between September 2005 and July 2006, to evalu ate the prospects of integrating the system with the clinical process, Our trials showed that a mobile health monitoring system can easily co-exist with other forms of service delivery by supplementing them or replacing previous practices. Indeed, a project partner, the Netherlands Medisch Spectrum Twente, noted the system s potential economic benefits and feasibility at low costs, besides healthcare delivery benefits in monitoring high risk pregnancies, another, Spain s the Hospital Clínic Provincial de Barcelona, Spain, the excellent results obtained with the use of HS24. The hospital used the system to support remote care during home-visits to aged and chronically ill patients with Chronic Obstructive Pulmonary Disease (COPD). Interestingly, according to Weingartner, Professionals have concluded that the system could easily be applied to their current work practices We learned a very important lesson. The process of incorporating a mobile monitoring solution is more of a socio-technical nature. Technology alone is not enough. This underscores the need to buy-in the end -user of these and other technologies for them not only to embrace the technologies, but also to use and keep using them, an important aspect of which is our discussion here on the new healthcare ICT that are available or would be, to doctors, and indeed, other healthcare professionals. Promoting the acquisition and use of these technologies by healthcare professionals is crucial to the derivation from the technologies of their immense benefits to the professional duties of these individuals that of healthcare delivery and to that they owe their societies and countries, which is to deliver qualitative health services cost-effectively. Indeed, the achievement of these dual healthcare delivery objectives is in the best interests of all, which is ascertainable on consideration of the the big picture , literally. The varieties of new wireless internet technologies emerging that could trim down doctor/hospital visits for patients with chronic diseases such as diabetes, heart failure, and mental illnesses, attest to the growing interest in mobile and wireless technologies, based on the realization of their immense potential in healthcare delivery. That they could enable the constant monitoring of millions of individuals with these chronic conditions remotely, and virtually, as they go about their daily routines, no doubt has the potential to save lives and reduce morbidities, improving overall health and reducing healthcare costs. Technologies by firms such as Abbott Laboratories, Medtronic, and Boston Scientific will, enable the monitoring and regulation of heart rate and delivery of shocks as required, wireless Internet doctor/patient communication, monitoring of blood, blood pressure, and weight, and could send alerts/reminders regarding cardiac/lung conditions, among others. These technologies essentially make it possible to reconstruct events that result in patients visiting the ER, but in the process, reduce hospitalization stays and rates, medications usage and costs, hence reduce overall health spending. A recent U.S Department of Veterans Affairs study followed 70 patients over three months, remotely monitoring their heart implants, which it found cut down the time their doctors would have sp ent on office visits by as many as eight days. In countries such as the U.S., financial concerns by doctors about collecting and reviewing patient data/information could hinder the adoption of these technologies, potentially, as many health insurers currently provide little if any reimbursement for them 1. This underlines the need to address all such issues relevant to the adoption of technologies that offer such great opportunities for achieving the dual healthcare delivery goals, for example litigation based on ascribing to doctors legal obligations for identifying warning signs. This is more so as doctors currently rely on data collection services that the device firms and autonomous monitoring services run to alert them of problems that might warrant prom pt medical attention. Mobile computing is going to be important to the future of healthcare delivery, both from the perspective of the healthcare provider and of the consumer. Doctors are mobile professionals, and need to be able to access patient data and information at the point of care (POC,) as an essential element of the efforts to deliver qualitative healthcare, access wireless computing provides, offering healthcare organizations, the litheness crucial to computerize their mobile healthcare professionals, fostering information communication, and sharing among professionals in disparate locations. In effect, this improves the quality of healthcare delivery, and in particular, as in the instances mentioned earlier regarding the treatment of chronic illnesses on an ambulatory/domiciliary basis, also empowers the healthcare consumer and makes it possible for the frail and elderly to receive care in the comfort of their homes, and with the support of family members. This is an important dimension for a grou p of patients who might not have much longer to live, but ensuring the best quality of life (QOL) for whom nonetheless is important. The devices available to doctors that tap into wireless capabilities are not just increasing in numbers but also in sophistication. Many doctors currently use personal digital assistants (PDAs) as Palm Pilots or Pocket PCs, the portability of these devices though, tempered by the compromised efficiencies of their relatively small screen sizes, which makes substantial data/information entry a chore in their use for patient management. The technicalities of wireless application development for PDAs are significant, including developers having to spray data elements out to the small viewer in correctly sized chunks, and not just reduce font size, and users to experience identical data flow display as the parent application, small memory a problem here too. Nonetheless, these devices are useful for short notes and data entry, and doctors could download valuable databases on them, for example, medications database offering crucial information on a variety of medications including the indications for their use, dosages, side effects, and interactions with other medications, and other things, among others. Laptops and notebooks have larger screens, but are heavier and less portable, consume significant power hence need regular recharging, necessitating downtime that could potentially compromise care delivery, and are prone to malicious logic. Security concerns are perhaps the most important in the health industry regarding these devices, with unauthorized access to patient information already a major hindrance to the widespread adoption of healthcare information and communication technologies, not even the Wired Encryption Privacy (WEP) adopted in 1999, as an aspect of the IEEE 802.11 standard, helping to allay these concerns. Experts have picked up major flaws in the WEP, developed to provide security to wireless networks akin to that wired networks have, hence the new standard, Wi-Fi Protected Access (WPA), which fortifies the encryption and user authentication process, offering better data/information security. For the use of PDAs, which many doctors incidentally already have, to become more widespread in healthcare delivery, and there is no doubt that even being able to access medications and diagnostic databases and patient information at the point of care (POC), could help save lives, healthcare organizations and their ICT units will have to take some major decisions. They would have to decide, for example, on whether their doctors should use devices that the organizations provided or their own. The latter case would increase the risks of viruses from remote devices attacking the organizations networks, risks that these organizations w ould need to weigh for example in the U.S. in keeping with HIPAA regulations, against the costs of providing all doctors, and other healthcare professionals as the case might be with laptops/notebooks, PDAs, and other handhelds. Considering the potential value of these devices in healthcare delivery, and the enormous markets out there for them, the onus seems to be on wireless application developers to build systems capable of scanning and inoculating viruses on remote devices, and applications that could d elete any patient data/information on stolen, lost, or compromised devices. Despite issues regarding decisions on device selection and network access, and on the flaws of the mobile devices themselves mentioned earlier, no doubt, in particular with newer technologies addressing these issues that healthcare organizations would increasingly deploy wireless networks to facilitate the collection, processing, and utilization of patient data/information by their mobile healthcare professionals at the POC. Doctors would increasingly have to use their cell phones for other than making calls, and other mobile/wireless devices for patient data entry, even if light and data access to fully integrated health information systems, among other healthcare delivery-related tasks. With the team approach to healthcare delivery gaining increasing currency, the need for more efficient and effective information dissemination and sharing among team members is even more urgent, and healthcare ICT, including wireless networks are going to be crucial aspects of realizing this enhanced connectivity.

Patient safety has taken center stage in healthcare delivery in recent times and decision support systems (DSS) play an important role in this regard. Clinical decision support systems come in various kinds, have different levels of functionalities, and even bear different names, for examples, advanced clinical decision support systems, or advanced clinical management systems. Computerized physician order entry (CPOE) for example, could simp ly involve entry of orders, and allergy or medications interactions checks, whereas mid - level systems might have additional features for examples, user preferences, and display options, with guided or mentored ordering, formulary integration, and costs optimization, among others possible with more advanced systems. All of these system levels, however, offer opportunities for medical error elimination such as those due to illegible handwritings, and dosage errors. Order management systems are likely to become even more sophisticated and to cater for both management and clinical needs, separately, or simultaneously. Solo practices and healthcare practitioners that combine their clinical work with some measure of practice management would increasingly find systems that could combine both functionalities more cost effective to implement, vendors also likely to respond to the demand that would ensue. Order/supply management in the practice management domain for example, more concerned with order/inventory tracking, shipping, receiving, picking, putaway, and resource deployment would among others increasingly use radio frequency ID (RFID) technologies, and bar code scanners, integrated with legacy ERP/procurement systems by some healthcare organizations. This again underscores the significant roles that wireless technologies would increasingly play in the health sector. Physicians with limited financial resources to invest on healthcare ICT would likely be keener on solutions that integrate these functionalities with at least certain aspects of their clinical order management, for example, able to track the use and ensure the accuracy of prescriptions, both that would likely be of interest to the relevant health plan in say the United States. Emerging clinical order management technologies utilize artificial intelligence in knowledge management to offer actionable data and information, usability and relevance even grouped for example into specialties, hospital or service types, tailoring decision support data/information to specific needs, enhancing the potential value of such information, including in assuring patient safety. Newer technologies would be able therefore to anticipate the clinical needs of doctors that would enable them ensure patient safety and offer them the tools that would facilitate the realization of these goals. In other words, newer technologies would not just be presenting the required data and information, customized to the particular end -user, or to the group that the end -user belongs, as the tw o might not in fact always coalesce, but would present the information in the preferred format, facilitating its use, thereby fostering patient safety. It would become increasingly clear to vendors that their products would sell more, if at all, to clientele that intends to use them, and not just needs them and to health organizations, developing products that are not just innovative, with smoother learning curves, but also user-friendly. It would also be clearer to the health system as a whole that the end -user, specifically doctors, and other healthcare professionals need to use even implemented systems for the achievement of the dual healthcare delivery goals to materialize. The development of DSS, for example, EMRs and CPOEs based on these principles would encourage their acquisition by doctors and their implementation in full, as many doctors only partially implement these technologies, hence not deriving their full benefits, and indeed, promote their usage. It would also likely eliminate some of the common complaints doctors currently have such as that these technologies compromise their productivity, which many experts believe partly explains some of the recent adverse research findings of these technologies2, 3. In an article in the Journal of the American Medical Association, Dr. Ross Koppel and colleagues noted the Role of Computerized Order Entry Systems in Facilitating Medication Errors 13. This report from the University Of Pennsylvania School Of Medicine based on an interview and survey-based stud y that described doctors observations of how a production computerized provider order entry (CPOE) system apparently resulted in medical errors, no doubt is troubling. Indeed, in another report in the May 23, 2005 issue of the Archives of Internal Medicine, Dr. Nebeker from the Salt Lake City Health Care System noted that adverse drug events rates persisted despite regular CPOE system use3. These studies underline the need for the appropriate deployment of these technologies, including fostering end -user adoption paying attention to the principles mentioned earlier. Comments Koppel and co underscored this point in the JAMA study mentioned above by their observation that a common problem leading to medical errors occurred at occasions of clinician handoffs, reported in previous studies in non-automated clinical settings4, 5,. This suggests that involving doctors in the design and configuration of these technologies early in their life cycles could have preempted many of the problems that the study noted, a situation implementing new technologies should clearly pursue. With the increasing emphasis on consumer-driven healthcare delivery, healthcare ICT would play an even larger role that would be difficult if not impossible without the widespread adoption of these technologies, which in turn depends in the main on their adoption by doctors and other healthcare professionals. It is therefore important that we continue to promote the adoption of these technologies by healthcare professionals, which in fact would stimulate individual and collaborative efforts to develop novel and inventive healthcare ICT, as vendors jostle for market share, and healthcare professionals, to create distinctive value propositions for increasingly technologically suave and financially prudent healthcare consumers. This is not to mention the pressure from payers a 2004 the Henry J. Kaiser Family Foundation and Health Research and Education Trust survey on employer health benefits in the U.S showing employers of 40% of the commercially insured population potentially offering health savings account plans by 2006, thanks to health insurers promotion to employers. Issues such as price lists for hospital procedures, physician reimbursement, for example, determining criteria for the pay-for-performance (P4P) model, and issues relating to it such as contesting charges, dissolution of the provider/ client location gap, Internet consultations, and cross-border credentialing issues, and the increasing public interest in patient safety are potential drivers of healthcare ICT adoption. These and other issues also call for the implementation of cutting-edge healthcare ICT to resolve/actualize them, hence are potential drivers of healthcare ICT innovation too. Healthcare organizations with brick and mortar bias for example, would have to rethink their corporate strategies with the increasing emphasis on ambulatory and domiciliary care, in particular on losing patronage hence need to leverage their competences to remain economically viable. This could for example mean increased off-shoring/ outsourcing to curtail costs, or in fact, the pursuit of more cross-border opportunities for volume gain, either of which strategy would require significant focus on healthcare ICT investments, specifically on novel technologies that could reverse the organization s fortunes. Such organizations might also want to leverage their current investments, exploiting scale economies and acquiring other related and smaller organizations to establish a regional or national network, which again would likely inspire the development of novel network and other healthcare ICT, proprietary or otherwise, to facilitate overall operations. Healthcare organizations are using eICU technologies to offer specialist services across borders, even across countries, and healthcare providers are re-inventing themselves into health and wellness agents and advisors, again, the need to offer better services regarding convenience and costs in particular besides quality, necessitating the sort of service/product differentiation that deploying appropriate healthcare ICT would engender. Retail health services and subscription health services provision are also spawning the development and use of novel technologies for example coded access card, prepayment cards, personal health records (PHR), web-based, or stored in a potable USB memory device, for example, and a variety of multimedia patient/doctor interactive technologies including audio/video monitoring that enable real-time patient evaluation and treatment. Progress in healthcare ICT would no doubt, further improve our capabilities regarding qualitative health services provision, which is in keeping with the customer-centred healthcare model gaining currency in many health jurisdictions, and would facilitate whose achievement of the dual healthcare delivery goals. The virtual or eICU for example is helping improve patient safety, reduce nosocomial or hospital acquired infections, complications, hence reduce the duration of hospitalization, saving costs in many hospitals in the U.S. that have strengthened their intensive care units (ICU) with the virtual or eICU facilities. Visicu -made virtual eICU for example, enables doctors to monitor all ICU patients from five computer screens in a command center not necessarily on hospital grounds, and indeed, could be far away. The eICU center gathers a variety of data for examples patients vital signs, even a slight decrease in blood oxygen or hemoglobin levels, dilated pupils or a patient about to fall off his/her bed via a number of cameras, videoconferencing equipment and computer software installed at his/her bedside. It feeds these data to the command center, the on-call doctor at the eICU able to alert doctors and nurses on the ground on required intercessions. An expert could actually supervise surgical procedures remotely using this technology, sitting in front of a computer screen perhaps thousands of kilometers away dictating the procedure to follow to another doctor with less experience who is performing the operation. The expert is able to monitor every move the other doctor performing the operation makes, via a high-resolution video camera and receive instant sensor data from say a catheter used in the procedure.

This example points to the need also for continuous broadband connection for uninterrupted real-time information communication and sharing as delay in data transmission on pressure inside the heart, say during a potentially life-saving cardiac catheterization using this technology could be disastrous. In other words, it shows that high-speed Internet access is not a luxury in contemporary healthcare delivery but in fact, a necessity, hence the need not just for cutting edge research on broadband technologies, but also for the political will to remove the bottlenecks in the way of the optimization of the potential of these technologies. In the U.S for example, despite its abundance of backbone bandwidth, capable of moving data across the country instantaneously, the high- speed networks slow considerably at the notorious the last mile , that is, the local connections linking homes and businesses to the Internet6. Federal Communications Commission Chairman Michael Powell in a speech in May 2005 aptly put the importance broadband technologies, when he said, If the United States is going to maintain its ability to grow its economy, I think the continued proliferation of broadband technologies is key to that solution This is the central communication policy objective of the era. It is more than talk now. It is time for action. This holds true for other countries as well. We need to be able to provide mobile high -speed data, video and audio feeds to our healthcare professionals at the point of care, including to emergency treatment personnel at the scene of an accident, say a road traffic accident, for which emerging technologies are already available, and which some health organizations have actually deployed. Other technologies are broadening the scope of Telemedicine , which has long been one of the most important high-speed networks applications, making it even more efficient to provide qualitative health services to our folks in rural and outlying areas, whose hospitals and clinics if available, in general lack access to the expertise/ experience of doctors in urban healthcare facilities. Telehealth technologies are ever more sophisticated and would be increasingly useful in the developed world for example to reach many of its elderly citizens no longer able to visit their doctors, even those living in u rban centers. In Spain, Italy, and Denmark for examples, experts are using a telecounselling service that the EU-sponsored HEALTH OPTIMUM project developed in 2005, that is assisting to set in motion the implementation of telemedicine across Europe. This Internet-based service even has a telelaboratory component enabling the remote analysis of patients test samples, overall with the system, doctors delivering even better, and experts services, and saving time doing so, patients receiving qualitative services in the comfort of their homes, and not having to travel in winter s harsh weather and treacherous roads, for examples. The health system also is able to achieve its dual healthcare delivery goals. Furthermore, because the patients GP is present during the videoconference consultation, patient care is better coordinated, the GP and the specialist able to study patient data together, including scans and samples, and plan management approaches. Developments in broadband technologies would no doubt continue to improve the use of high-quality audio/video and of real- time data connections between remote and urban facilities, facilitating remote consultation, diagnosis, and treatment, as the example of Visicu s technological integration of audio, visual, and clinical data shows. This indeed, is a significant achievement in the health sector, noted for its myriad of disparate, silo-like applications and systems, such as lab and pharmacy systems, bought from different vendors and often not interoperable. Besides the complexity of working with these different systems, and the difficulty in optimizing their potentials, they incur significant running and maintenance costs, essentially operating counter to the dual healthcare delivery objectives viewed strictly, hence the need for such technologies as the eICU that provide qualitative care, and help reduce health spending in the process. According to Peter Angood, vice president of the Joint Commission on Accreditation of Healthcare Organizations, Health care has been in a period of tight financial constraints for years and institutions are often hesitant to make large investments Obviously, technology has been expensive. There needs to be a strong return on investment , a bill he noted the eICU appears to fit7. There are indeed, prospects for financial returns on these technologies, not just for the networking industry, but also by the entire country, an estimated $300 billion to $500 billion a year to the U.S. economy by broadband technologies for example, and accord ing to a Brookings Institution study, 1.2 million jobs in the country courtesy of widespread broadband access18. Critical Care Medicine noted that at Sentara Healthcare, eICU led to a 27% reduction in hospital mortality among patients in the ICU, a 17% decrease stay lengths, and a $2,150 per patient costs savings, a total of $3 million savings over the eICU costs18. One hospital reduced by over 50% its incidence of ventilator-associated pneumonia, or VAP, which increases the chances of patients dying by 50%, and costs the hospital $40,000 in extended hospital stays and sundry care. The benefits of broadband and other technologies are indeed, immense, and in particular by enhancing the capability of our first responders, would help save lives and hospital costs, not to mention disease burden, hence the need for the political will to e set aside even-more wireless spectrum for public health and safety. A expert could establish say atelepathology practice, providing services to hospitals far away, the expert s computer fed video images from a remote-controlled microscope in the other hospitals via a broadband connection, with which he/she would diagnose cancers and other diseases in tissue samples. Doctors could also swap large data files for examples X-rays that do not require real-time connections although still require high-speed networks, and healthcare organizations utilize broadband technologies in non-life-threatening situations too, saving significant labor and other resources for example utilizing these technologies to process medical claims, insurance, and a variety of other administrative functions. Broadband also would play an increasing role in ambulatory and domiciliary care. Patients treated at home could communicate with their doctors via videoconferences and other technologies, with the potential for considerable costs savings. With broadband speeds increasing, some experts suggesting we need up to 100mbps or more to the home for this to happen, talk of a broadband revolution not just in healthcare delivery, but indeed, in all other aspects of our lives, a sort of cultural revolution, is in the air, literally. This is more so considering the pace of progress in 3G, satellite, wi-fi and other wireless technologies, many of these technologies with significant potential for applications in healthcare delivery. Experts also contend that the healthcare industry would increasingly need to embrace a service-oriented ICT architecture to facilitate the realization of an interoperable electronic health records (EHR) system as the healthcare consumer increasingly becomes pivotal. This is, as in particular the consumer-centricity of contemporary healthcare delivery would require for example the development of portal frameworks or other technologies by healthcare organizations to publish pricing information on health services and procedures to the POC. This would mean that the customary tripartite architecture layers of hardware, enterprise systems, and workflow applications are no longer adequate and need an extra layer added to accommodate increased/ fluctuant user loads. Coupled with the likely increasing use of thin clients for web development to preempt problems with speed and bandwidth, these issues would make the development of the extra service architecture increasingly imperative in healthcare delivery in the future. An important aspect of the emergence of new healthcare ICT to meet changing healthcare needs, is the issue of information security, and is one which no doubt would novel technologies in the near future, for example, the increasing use e- signature, such as the digital signature, which cryptographically and uniquely links the signer s identity to a document. Versus generic electronic signature that might lack security features and a qualified certificate, digital signatures would help secure patient information, and reassure patients of this safety. It would therefore help increase the prospects of widespread healthcare ICT adoption by healthcare providers as the public increasingly trust that private health information communicated and shared by doctors and other healthcare providers do not end up the wrong hands. These developments and emerging technologies will shape the future of healthcare delivery, and with the Internet projected to be a thriving, low -cost network of billions of devices by 2020, according to a recent key survey of leading technology experts, the Pew report on the future internet, the options for health services delivery would be as varied as they are sophisticated. The Pew Internet and American Life report sought canvassed opinions from the experts on seven broad scenarios about the future internet, based on recent developments in Internet technology, experts predicting that many more of present day s 10 billion new embedded m icros annually will be on the Internet8. Others predict the dominance of the mobile Internet, access tools mostly mobile, with most mobile networks offering one-gigabit-per-second- minimum speed, anywhere, anytime, although some expressed concerns regarding interoperability, privacy, security, government regulation, and commercial interests hindering the widespread adoption of emerging Internet technologies. With regard privacy and security, the significant roles hackers and eco-terrorists would play in attempting to thwart progress would be crucial in the health industry, which would therefore need to be a step ahead of these malicious groups, with regard the technologies needed to counter their efforts. This is more so as with improvements in broadband technologies and in Internet technologies for example regarding the semantic web mentioned earlier, and the accompanying increase in the numbers of persons with access to the Internet, living and working in virtual worlds essentially, would be more opportunities for health services delivery online. In essence, healthcare providers should be ready to follow the future healthcare consumer in and out of the real world complete with the implications for both health and health services delivery, specifically a better understanding of the healthcare needs of the next generation of humans and of the best ways to meet these needs.

The varieties of healthcare information and communication technologies that would be significant players, in future healthcare delivery are legion. E- prescribing for example, for which doctors in the U.S. for example receive P4P inducements, and essentially comprises confirming pharmacy benefit eligibility, enforcing the formulary, reporting on drug history, and channeling prescriptions to a retail/mail order pharmacy, is gaining currency. However, despite the potential of these technologies to reduce medical errors, and save lives and money, concerns such as compromised productivity and costs, linger on. At an average cost of between $1,500 and $10,000, and another $1000 to $3,000 to implement in the first and second years, respectively, costs dependent on the nature, and functionalities of the legacy practice management systems of the doctor s office, and its Internet connectivity, wireless access, learning curves, patient data loading, and licenses, among others, they are not exactly cheap. Then there are maintenance costs, and costs of upgrades, all, good reasons to support doctors in acquiring and implementing these valuable technologies, particularly those in solo practices with tight budgets for healthcare ICT. Such support would contribute significantly to our efforts to promote the widespread use of these and other healthcare ICT among doctors, and indeed, by extension, among other healthcare stakeholders, and to achieve the dual healthcare delivery goals. Besides its use in supply chain management mentioned earlier RFID deployment is becoming commonplace even in clinical settings. No doubt, they are valuable technologies in particular as emphasis has moved from enterprise systems, hitherto focused on automating execution, for examples, order processing, invoices, and other such discrete transactions in an overt drive to improve operations and reduce costs9, toward the development of new technologies to improve manufacturing resource planning, including emphasis on logistical operations/supply chain management. In other words, there is increasing emphasis on decomposing the issues involved healthcare delivery, revealing their underlying su b-issues and processes, in a continuous decomposition/exposition cycle, which would reveal the appropriate technologies to implement in improving the processes and resolving the problems pertaining to these issues. RFID or radio frequency identification has tiny microchips, smaller than a grain of sand, with antennae on them, and is capable of transmitting a unique code or other data to an RFID reader wirelessly, via radio transmission. The technology currently widely deployed in retailers' supply chains, stuck to pallets, crates, and stock, working like electronic barcodes, obviating the need for manual counting of stock items, waving an RFID reader near the tag, which can read the chips as far away as 10 feet, only necessary for all the counting and stock identification required. RFID chips currently have increasing applications in supermarket loyalty cards, banknotes, on clothes and pharmaceuticals, and even inside credit cards and passports. Because the reader could only read tags at short distances, the technology would unlikely have any significant surveillance value, a concern among some, to which proponents counter that even then, retailers could disable the chips as soon as shoppers leave a store and should give consumers the option to refuse having their purchases tagged. Despite these concerns and others for examples about the chips being costly to put on every pallet, much more every stock item, and the technology s lacks of standards, it is gaining increasing currency in the health sector. Its uses include tracking instruments, especially those in short supply and shared by different medical/nursing units, ensuring the right patient is in the surgical theater for the right surgery, and to track ill, and elderly disoriented patients, among others, and in automating certain processes and repetitive tasks. In effect, RFID is helping to provide safer, more efficient care to patients, simultaneously savings costs, the process cycle analyses mentioned above opening even more potential areas of RFID deployment in the over healthcare delivery process, for example tracking medical supplies use, integrated into suppliers information systems for automatic replacement of used supplies when they fall behold a threshold. With hospital services continuing to guzzle significant portions of health systems funds, in the U.S., a third, about 33% of every dollar spent on U.S. health care going toward inpatient hospital care, according to a recent HHS s Agency for Healthcare Research and Quality, report, the need to revisit health services delivery is no doubt urgent10. In 2004, federal and state governments for Medicare and Medicaid reimbursements, received over 60% of hospital bills, or $475 billion out of $790 billion, excluding physician fees, Medicare billed $363 billion, or 46% of hospital bills, and Medicaid, $112 billion, or 14.1 % of hospital bills, hospital charges to private insurers were $252 billion, almost a third of all bills. Should we indeed, not embrace healthcare ICT that could reduce these costs, while assuring the delivery of qualitative health services under these circumstances, particularly considering that $44 billion, nearly 6% of total hospital bills was for treating coronary atherosclerosis? Does this not in fact make even more sense considering the costs of this most expensive condition to treat but whose prevalence primary prevention could reduce and whose treatment could be ambulatory and to accomplish which these technologies could help immensely? Could we also not reduce the hospital stays related to treating pregnant women and delivering babies, which was second costliest, $41 billion, and in fact for newborn and mother stays, the two most expensive for Medicaid, and indeed, for others such as Schizophrenia, the fourth most expensive condition for Medicaid, and depression and bipolar disorder, the fifth for examples? As the report noted, As health care costs rise and the population ages, policymakers are concerned with the growing burden of hospital-based medical care and expenses to government, consumers and insurers,   and rightfully so, and which underscores the points made earlier about the need to implement the healthcare ICT that could help in achieving the dual healthcare delivery objectives. This applies not just to the U.S health systems but also to all health jurisdictions, most if not all confronting similar ballooning healthcare costs. It also underscores the point about the link between issues in healthcare delivery and their potential to spawn innovative healthcare information and communication technologies as process cycle analyses reveal the issues and processes to address and the appropriate healthcare ICT with which so to do, in our quest to achieve the dual healthcare delivery goals. In Canada, for example, recent Organization for Economic Co- operation and Development (OECD) annual health data statistics showed that Canadians make more out-of-pocket payments than their typical counterparts in other OECD countries do. In 2004, out-of-pocket payments and private insurance was 30% of Canadian health care spending, about 3% over the OECD average, 27%11, 13% of healthcare bill in the country private-insurance paid, versus the 6.5% OECD average, although out-of-pocket payments was 15% of total health bill of Canadians, versus the 20% OECD average. The differences most marked with drugs, private payments 62% of Canada s overall drug bill, versus 39%, OECD average, and 88% and 76% for Mexico and the U.S., respectively, or 11% for Ireland, the least are instructive. So are that private insurance health care expenses have been increasing in the past 15 years, public share, now below the OECD average of 71.6%, 69.8% in 2004, versus 74.5% in 1990, as table 1 shows.

Table 1: Public share of total health expenditures in OECD countries

Country	% of total expenditures on health	
	1990	2004
Australia	67.1	--
Austria	73.5	70.7
Belgium	--	--
Canada	74.5	69.8
Czech Republic	97.4	89.2
Denmark	82.7	--
Finland	80.9	76.6
France	76.6	78.4
Germany	76.2	--
Greece	53.7	52.8
Hungary	--	72.5
Iceland	86.6	83.4
Ireland	71.9	79.5
Italy	79.1	76.4
Japan	77.6	--
Korea	38.5	51.4
Luxembourg	93.1	90.4
Mexico	40.4	46.4
Netherlands	67.1	62.3
New Zealand	82.4	77.4
Norway	82.8	83.5
Poland	91.7	68.6
Portugal	65.5	71.9
Slovak Republic	--	--
Spain	78.7	70.9
Sweden	89.9	84.9
Switzerland	52.4	58.4
Turkey	61.0	72.1
United Kingdom	83.6	85.5
United States	39.7	44.7
Average	72.8	71.6

Note: OECD = Organisation for Economic Co-operation and Development.
Source: OECD Health Data, June 2006.

Private insurance payments in Canada increased from about 8.1% in the early 1990s to almost 13% in 2004, versus 6.5%, OECD average, and of that Australia that fell 11.4% to 7.4%. The country spent 9.9% of its GDP in 2004 on health, a percentage point more than the OECD average of 8.9%, less than the U.S., which spent 15.3%, and Switzerland, Germany and France, which allocated 10.5% or more of their GDP to healthcare that year12. Canada ranks higher than the OECD average in total health spending per capita, US$3165 in 2004 (adjusted for purchasing power parity), versus US$2550, OECD average. Do these figures not indicate the need for Canada to find ways to reduce health spending while simultaneously delivering qualitative health services, particularly as it would likely be spending more of its GDP on health as its population ages, and considering the trend of the proportion of health expenses private insurance bears? Would the country therefore not need to intensify efforts to promote the widespread diffusion of healthcare ICT? Would the d evelopment of innovative healthcare ICT services and products not be a necessary accompaniment of these promotional efforts? Do these figures not also exemplify the need for the process cycle analyses mentioned earlier to reveal the underlying issues and p rocesses in the country s health system that these technologies could help resolve and facilitate respectively, making the achievement of the dual healthcare delivery goals even likelier? This example also shows the need for other countries to engage in su ch analyses as part of the efforts to understand in-depth, their respective health systems, and their peculiar problems, a thorough exploration that would also reveal appropriate solutions, hence the realization of their healthcare delivery objectives.

Still in Canada, a new the Canadian Institute for Health Information (CIHI), study, The Evolving Role of Canada's Fee-for-Service Family Physicians, 1994 to 2003 that updates a 2004 report stressing provincial data in nine clinical areas for fee- for service family physicians noted that they are offering less obstetrical care and inpatient care13. The number of family physicians providing obstetrical care reduced by almost 50% since 1994, of male doctors doing so by 12.8%, and of female doctors, by 11.3% between 1994 and 2003. The number of family doctors in rural areas providing hospital inpatient care fell from 80% to 75% in the same period, 61% and 48%, for urban doctors, respectively during the same period. Noted Dr. Louise Nasmith, president of the College of Family Physicians of Canada Our college was not surprised by the findings The system has become more and more fragmented, and it is harder for doctors to access the care that they need from specialists. It makes it difficult to provide a seamless p ractice. Added Nasmith While there are more family physicians in urban areas, doctors in rural areas are more likely to provide full-service care, as a result, they are burning out quickly, because they are on call all the time, which, along with the earlier observations attest to the need for the sort of decomposition/exposition exercise mentioned earlier. They also call for the employment of the integrative potential of healthcare information and communication technologies in resolving the specific und erlying issues and processes of these problems, including for example, exploring the prospects of telehealth and some of the other technologies mentioned earlier as deemed relevant. Again, this example brings to the fore, the need for such exercises in other health jurisdictions, which as earlier noted, would have their specific issues to address, hence also the difficulty in a cure-all prescription of healthcare ICT even for the same health jurisdiction. These examples also show the fundamental interplay between healthcare information and communication technologies and healthcare delivery, progress in either, essentially symbiotic. Consider for example the recent decision by IBM announced on September 26, 2006 plans of a new line of product bundles comprising hardware, software and technical assistance in a bid to boost sales to small and medium -sized firms (SMEs), 30 such bundles billed for release over a two month period 14. IBM plans to in troduce standardized products that customers could order via a catalog, for building an information technology infrastructure as part of IBM s plans to expand services sales among small and medium-size firms unable to afford to contract IBM to design customized IT systems. This is a plan from which solo medical practices and other healthcare providers with limited IT budgets would no doubt benefit. IBM's services business has customarily focused on bigger firms, laden with the financial wherewithal to fund labor-intensive IT projects that IBM engineers manage, but this latest move by the company offers smaller firms, including in the health sector, the opportunity to acquire and implement cutting-edge healthcare ICT at affordable prices. This is clearly an important contribution by IBM to the efforts to promote healthcare ICT diffusion, and ultimately to achieve the dual healthcare delivery goals. IBM has already announced two product bundles for example that would help firms implement communications networks supporting data, voice, and video. In the next few weeks, the company plans to release bundles for digital video surveillance and for services-oriented architecture that facilitate collaboration among dissimilar computer systems, both as we noted earlier, critical to creating the enabling milieu for the sort of process improvement necessary for the achievement of the dual healthcare delivery goals. This example underlines the symbiotic relationship between healthcare ICT and progress in healthcare delivery mentioned above, and by extension, the importance of promoting innovation and creativity in both domains that would eventually feed into each other, enhancing both in perpetuity, fostering the achievement of the dual healthcare delivery objectives in like manner. It is likely that other major ICT firms would follow IBM s example considering the size of the potential market out there, which if so would augur well for the SMEs on the one hand, including in the health industry as earlier noted, where, on the other, it would in fact, also create immense opportunities for the entire health system. This is because not only would the smaller healthcare providers be able t afford ICT that could hitherto not afford, market forces would actually force down prices over time as more large firms foray into the markets, making healthcare ICT increasingly affordable, and its diffusion, hence more widespread. Furthermore, because the more diffused these technologies are, the likelier would be the chances of realizing the dual objectives mentioned earlier, it makes the efforts to realize the ubiquity of healthcare ICT not just worth pursuing, but actually intensifying. With the many challenges facing contemporary health systems, which would likely worsen were they not to take the necessary measures to address them, the future of healthcare delivery is indeed going to be crusty. We need to come to terms with the value that implementing healthcare ICT could bring to the transition of health services delivery, to make the road less bumpy. This does not mean that we should implement these technologies willy- nilly. On the other hand, each healthcare provider and health jurisdiction needs first to determine which of the technologies it needs based on thorough process cycle analyses, for example, in the context of a wider quest to advance quality in healthcare delivery, and affordably too. In other words, we should aim for the best quality in healthcare ICT to obtain the best value in healthcare delivery. This would not necessarily occur acquiring the latest innovative technologies, from which we would not obtain any real value in addressing our particular healthcare delivery problems. On the other hand, we need to invest in healthcare ICT that would move our health jurisdiction toward improving health services and care delivery, and simultaneously redu cing healthcare costs. We need to implement technologies for example that would for example, help integrate clinical data, claims data and personalized care to facilitate decision making by the healthcare consumer on various aspects of his/her health, by d octors on appropriate and timely patient management and by payers, on reimbursement and related issues. No doubt, such technologies would offer multi-level authentication and assure the safety and security of patient information, and would most of all be interoperable with the variety of multi-vendor systems with which it would attempt to integrate seamlessly. Here again, we see the direction the interaction between healthcare ICT and healthcare delivery is likely heading in the future, one wherein, issues in one domain trigger developments in the other, in this instance, the development of the appropriate technologies to make the increasing shift in healthcare delivery toward consumer-centeredness, work. We would doubtless continue to see novel technologies emerge that support this integration of personal health records (PHR) for example with health care costs and quality data, among others, making the healthcare consumer more discerning, the healthcare provider, more attuned to healthcare consumer needs, including implementing the relevant healthcare ICT to meet them, and the healthcare-provider reimbursement system, more efficient. In the U.S., Medicare Web sites are already offering these integrated data sources, and attracting beneficiaries in droves, in the last year, CMS consumer Web sites registering 400 million page views, initial results showing that beneficiaries that use these personalized sites likelier use preventative services. This no doubt has implications for improving health and disease outcomes and for reducing health spending, essentially for the achievement of the dual healthcare delivery goals we have harped on so much thus far. Additionally, CMS pay-for-performance and e-prescribing pilot programs are driving system improvements that are changing how providers invest in healthcare information technology, noted Mark McClellan, the outgoing U.S. Medicare, recently. As noted above, individuals are paying increasingly more for their healthcare not just in Canada, but also in many other countries. In the U.S., for example, health insurance premiums for employer-sponsored health coverage has been increasing, by an average 7.7% in 2006, for example, even if not as much as the 9.2% increase in 2005 or the recent 13.9% peak in 200315. While this year showed the slowest premium growth rate since 2000, they still rose over twice as fast as wages, 3.8%, and overall inflation, 3.5%. With premiums having hiked 87% since 2000, family health coverage now an average of $11,480 per year, and with workers paying $2,973 on the average toward premiums, roughly $1,354 over in 2000, should the healthcare consumer not be more discerning? With SMEs and their employees, essentially bearing the brunt of the healthcare coverage, two in five small businesses not even offering health insurance, those so doing, asking workers to contribute significantly more to their premiums for family coverage than before, the healthcare provider would in time have no choice but to work with them to reduce health spending. However, this would have to be while not compromising healthcare delivery, an indication of the likely need for these providers for distinctive value propositions to the healthcare consumer to sustain, let alone increase patronage in the face of stiff competition by other providers willing to deploy sophisticated healthcare ICT in such product/service differentiation. Here again, we see the interplay of developments in health service models, in this case the consumer-driven healthcare inspiring technological progress, and vice-versa. Enrollment in consumer-driven plans in the U.S., continues apace, albeit cautiously with 2.7 million workers enrolled in high-deductible plans that have a savings option, including plans qualified for health savings accounts (HSAs)15, roughly 4% of insured workers enrolled in plans of that sort. With these figures possibly increasing over the years, coverage for the 155 million Americans who depend on employer-sponsored health insurance thus more likely to fall under HSAs and other consumer-driven plans, the interplay between healthcare ICT innovation and healthcare delivery mentioned earlier would likely heighten.

To be sure, the estimated 4% of insured workers in the U.S., currently enrolled in high-deductible plans with a savings option, is much smaller than the 60% in preferred provider organizations (PPOs), 20% in health maintenance organizations (HMOs), 13% in point-of-service plans, and 3% in traditional indemnity plans. However, that high-deductible health plans with a savings option, for example, comprising HSA-qualified, and health reimbursement arrangement (HRA-related,) which about 7% of employers offer, are tax-favored accounts that employees could utilize to fund medical bills make the concept attractive. That these consumer-driven plans so termed because the health consumer pays directly for more portions of their healthcare expenses, hence would likely be more discerning in service utilization, enabling them to obtain high quality services at affordable costs would likely increase enrollment in these plans, and ultimately reduce and indeed, reverse the rising premium rates. Twelve percent of firms with 1,000 and more workers in the U.S offer an HSA- qualified plan. Furthermore, of the estimated 2.7 million workers enrolled in HSAs or HRAs in 2006, 1.4 million are in HSA-qualified plans versus 0.8 million in 2005, and in plans with HRAs, 1.3 million, no change statistically from 200515. At an average of $3,405 yearly for single coverage and $9,484 for family coverage, premiums for these plans are lower than for other health-plan types, partly due to more employee cost sharing, and excluding employer contributions to savings accounts, averagely $743 for single coverage and $1,359 for family coverage. Included, these contributions make overall health spending for these plans averagely similar to that for PPOs, the commonest plans, which is why some contend that employers might not embrace consumer-driven health plans en masse, after all, as savings from the plans overall might not offset consumer worries about higher cost sharing. The question remains though if employer- based insurance keep declining if the disparity between increasing premiums and workers purse continues, as more employers and workers would be unable to afford insurance coverage costs, or could we halt the decline. Many would likely respond to this question in the affirmative, but also to that regarding whether stemming this disparity providing workers qualitative care for less costs via deploying appropriate healthcare information and communication technologies would halt, even reverse the decline. Considering the large numbers of families that depend on employer-based health insurance, roughly 61% of firms in the country offering health benefits to at least some employees in 2006, almost all large firms, with 200 or more workers, less than 50% of the smaller firms, with 3-9 workers, it would no doubt be crucial for such insurance to persist. This means that it would be necessary to create the right atmosphere for this to happen, in particular which would encourage SMEs to offer coverage to more of their workers, considering that employees of small firms, with 3-199 employees, averagely contribute substantially more to their premiums, $3,550 for family coverage, than those in the bigger firms that contribute averagely, $2,658. This would include making the necessary readjustments to certain provisions of the relevant laws to make consumer-driven health plans for example, even more attractive to workers and their employees. Regardless of the approach to curtailing healthcare costs though, disease management, consumer-directed health plans, higher employer cost sharing, or stricter managed care networks, among others, the important role that healthcare ICT could play in achieving this goal is not in doubt. Nor is it, that of its potential to help achieve the goal simultaneously ensuring the delivery of qualitative health services. The question again is the intensity of the forces operating in each of these approaches in determining the willingness or otherwise to deploy these technologies by not just the healthcare provider, but also the healthcare consumer, and indeed, all the other stakeholders involved. In other words, would the approach not triumph in the end that is able to create the enabling environment for not only the widespread implementation of these technologies, but the maximization of their potential in helping achieve the dual healthcare delivery objectives? Would the success of each approach therefore not predicate on the healthcare consumer paying less for similar quality of healthcare? Would the efficiency of each approach to make this happen not depend on that of the interplay between the emergence of innovative healthcare information and communication technologies inspired by progress in healthcare delivery and vice versa? Would the momentum for any particular approach to gain ascendancy not depend on attaining the critical mass mandatory for the tipping point toward possibly unassailable competitive edge? The point here is that the future of healthcare delivery is in the hands of the healthcare consumer, whichever way one views it, as the consumer is the ultimate payer, again, whichever way one looks at the issues. Given this reality, the consumer will likely be keen, understandably, although there are in fact compelling economic reasons for its validity, on the realization of the dual healthcare delivery goals mentioned earlier, indeed, at both the individual and system levels. The realization of these goals at the individual level would require first for the healthcare consumer to have adequate, accurate, and current health-related information. In other words, the contemporary and future healthcare consumer would to seek to rectify the perennial information sym metry in the health sector rooted in the paternalistic atavism of the medical profession, which albeit with good intentions, falls short in a healthcare delivery age with new challenges. It would be hard for anyone to gainsay the role that healthcare ICT w ould play in this quest for information, let alone the benefits its achievement would confer on the ability of the healthcare consumer to be more discerning in service utilization, and on the provider in realizing competitive advantage via sophisticated ICT-backed, value propositions. The more suave the taste and expectation of the healthcare provider, the more that of the technologies involved in meeting them would likely be, again highlighting the interplay between progress in healthcare delivery and innovation in healthcare information and communication technologies. It is clear that besides facilitating the realization of the dual healthcare delivery goals at both individual and system levels, the dyadic of healthcare ICT and healthcare delivery ensures progress in both domains. The central role that doctors could play in this continuous process would be, not doubt gratifying, materially, and perhaps even more so, in the sense of being integral parts of the progress of humankind.

References

1. Available at: http://www.va.gov/ Accessed on September 22, 2006

2. Koppel R, Metlay JP, Cohen A, Abaluck B, Localio AR, Kimmel SE, Strom BL. Role of Computerized Physician Order Entry Systems in Facilitating Medication Errors. JAMA. 2005 Mar 9; 293(10):1197-203.

3. Nebeker JR, Hoffman JM, Weir CR, Bennett CL, Hurdle JF, High Rates of Adverse Drug Events in a Highly Computerized Hospital. Arch Intern Med. 2005 May 23; 165(10):1111-6.

4. Dowding D, examining the effects that manipulating information given in the change of shift report has on nurses care planning ability, Journal of Advanced Nursing, March 2001, Vol. 33 Issue 6 Page 836.

5. Petersen LA, Brennan TA, O Neil AC, Cook EF, Lee T. Does housestaff discontinuity of care increase the risk for preventable adverse events? Ann Intern Med. 1994 Dec 1; 121(11):866-7.

6. Available at: http://news.com.com/Broadband+A+life-saving+technology/2009- 1034_3-5261361.html? tag=nl Accessed on September 24, 2006

7. Available at: http://news.com.com/Hospitals+look+to+the+virtual+ICU/2100- 11393_3-5913059.html? tag=cd.hed Accessed on September 24, 2006

157

8. Available at:

http://newsvote.bbc.co.uk/mpapps/pagetools/print/news.bbc.co.uk/2/hi/technolo

gy/5370688.stm Accessed on September 24, 2006

9. O Brien, James A. (1996). Management Information Systems, 3rd Edition. Chicago: Times Mirror.

10. Available at:

http://www.kaisernetwork.org/daily_reports/rep_index.cfm?DR_ID=40018

11. Available at: http://www.cmaj.ca/cgi/content/full/175/7/729?etoc

12. Available at:

http://www.oecd.org/document/46/0,2340,en_2649_37407_34971438_1_1_1_37407

,00.html Accessed on September 25, 2006

13. Available at: http://www.cmaj.ca/cgi/content/full/175/7/728-a Accessed On September 15, 2006

14. Available at: http://news.com.com/2102-1022_3-6119453.html?tag=st.util.print Accessed on September 26, 2006

15. Available at:

http://content.healthaffairs.org/cgi/content/abstract/hlthaff.25.w476. Accessed on September 26, 2006

Changing Paradigms in Contemporary Healthcare Delivery

That as events in our world unfold we would have but no choice other than reevaluate our place in the cosmos is an understatement were we to remember the Kantian contrast between the beautiful and the sublime. The action to which the exigencies of a global milieu drive us, where the illness contracted in a remote Himalayan village could become a pandemic and transform the harmonious interplay of the imagination and reason we experience into conflict, our imposed perplexity the veritable wellspring of the ensuing vigor in us discovering our dignity and destiny, at once rends us. The need to jettison dated concepts of healthcare delivery therefore, needs no gainsaying. We realize the need for action intuitively, our individual and collective interests at stake otherwise. Speaking on September 26, 2006 at a conference sponsored by eHealth Initiative, a non-profit coalition of interest groups on health information technology, Intel Corp. chair Craig Barrett noted that the migration offshore of U.S. jobs would persist if corporate America did not exert its influence to compel the healthcare industry to adopt systems that will improve efficiency and reduce costs1. We would in our discussion term these two tasks the dual healthcare delivery goals. That same day, the Kaiser Family Foundation reported that health care premiums increased at a 7.7% yearly rate in 2005, twice that of consumer inflation2. With healthcare costs in the U.S. at an average of more than $6,000 per person in 2004, Barrett warned that Every job that can be moved out of the United States will be moved out ... because of health care costs. The Intel Corp. chair implored employers to demand that hospitals implement standardized record system s to reduce costs or move their firm s business somewhere else. Noting the difficulty due to soaring healthcare costs that U.S. companies increasingly have competing favorably in the global market, he added, The (health care) system is out of control, it s unstable, it s basically bankrupt, it gets worse each year and all we do is tinker around the edges when what we need are major fixes. He recommended standards such as full electronic patient records, and published best practices for patient management, which companies should seek in healthcare providers, which latter he noted should become competitive centres for excellence remunerated to sustain employees health, and which should compete for companies business offering qualitative yet low - cost treatment. To underscore Intel s commitment to these principles, it recently teamed up with other key industry players Cisco Systems Inc. and Oracle Corp. on a pilot program that recompensed health care providers for the quality care provided employees. Speaking at the same conference, Wal-Mart Stores Inc. Executive VP, Linda Dillman urged the health care industry to take a cue from her company, which uses computers to track every inventory item with resulting remarkable efficiency, to which Barret responded that Every other industry has adopted this technology and (the health care) industry continues to sit here and debate. No nation wants a flight of jobs overseas, its youths left roaming the streets aimlessly idleness generating a mix of confusion and mischief the brew shearing the fabric of the society, or whatever is left of it, whose future custodian they would inevitably be. Yet, we must temper our proclivity to romanticize customary Kantian relics in entirety, in particular not also oblivious to Moorean characterization of good as non-natural, in essence, non-empirical , the interlocking dyadic of the sublime and intuition, a compelling paradox with a motorized imperative, sufficient to transform an overwhelming moral experience into action. Act we must therefore, confronted as we were by Barrett with the facts, or if we did with those of the U.K., where in Budget 2002, the Chancellor announced the largest ever sustained spending growth in National Health Service s (NHS) history: £40 billion extra resources in the UK by 2007-08 versus 2002-03, an annual average growth of 7.3% above inflation3. Notably even that way back, government linked the resources to a package of reforms including devolution of resources and responsibility for delivery in instalments to local organizations, with the greatest freedoms and leeway to those highest performing, underpinned by the introduction of new performance improvement incentives, and emphasis on accountability, reinforced by increased patient choice. Table 1 shows estimated NHS spending between 2002 and 2008. Coupling investments with reform highlights the significance of the system

	£ million					
	2002-03	2003-04	2004-05	2005-06	2006-07	2007-08
Total UK NHS spending[1]	68,065	74,849	82,193	90,489	99,373	109,359
UK NHS estimated cash spending[2]	65,364	72,085	79,271	87,198	95,893	105,573

1 Full resource budgeting basis, net of depreciation. UK spending is subject to the decisions of the devolved administrations.

2 Consistent with previous control basis.

Table 1: U.K. NHS Spending: Source HM Treasury SR 2002: report3

working as it should to deliver qualitative health services, and cost-effectively, an approach endorsed by the Wanless Commission that in his 2001 Budget the Chancellor established to review the long-term trends and resource needs expected to influence the health service in the UK over the next two decades, part of efforts to sustain progress in healthcare delivery. The recommendations in the final report include an accent on the significance of a more productive and plastic workforce, more effective technology use, improved disease prevention and resource optimization, the achievement of all of which the deployment of appropriate healthcare ICT would doubtless facilitate. The report also anticipated an increase in health spending, in the first few years to offset previous under-investment, and in later years, the fully engaged scenario, one of three, projected to cost least and yield most and best health outcomes. Table 2 shows the projected percentage of the GDP that would fund healthcare delivery until 2008 and as with Table 1 earlier, which shows growth in health spending during the same period, the resources expected to help achieve the objectives of the Department of Health's new Public Service Agreement (PSA), including a new target maximum waiting time for hospital treatment of three months by 2008. Other targets include introducing booked appointments by 2005 to increase patient choice, addressing health inequalities, and drug abuse, reducing mortality rates from cancer and heart disease, and ER treatment wait times, and establishing new standards to help seniors live at home independently. Are projections for the future going to follow these patterns, and continue to increase in particular with the population aging and considering the potential dynamics of EU labor movement policies, among other factors? Between 1999 and 2004, health spending per capita in the U.K., increased averagely by 5.8% annually in real

	Per cent of GDP					
	2002-03	2003-04	2004-05	2005-06	2006-07	2007-08
Total UK health spending	7.7	8.0	8.3	8.7	9.0	9.4
of which						
Gross UK NHS spending[1]	6.6	6.9	7.2	7.5	7.8	8.2
Non-NHS health spending[2]	1.2	1.2	1.2	1.2	1.2	1.2

1 The NHS budget is net of certain receipts. To measure total health spending in line with the national accounts, total NHS spending is gross of these receipts and is on a near-cash basis.

2 Includes an additional 1.1 per cent of GDP for private spending on health, as assumed in the Wanless Report, as well as minor changes for charity spend and national accounts classifications. Total assumption for non-NHS spending is 1.15 per cent so some totals may not sum due to rounding.

Table 2: U.K health spending as a proportion of GDP: Source HM Treasury SR 2002: report3

terms, above OECD s 5.2% per annum average growth rate, and more than most other EU countries4. Indeed, it has increased progressively since the lull in the mid 1990s, when health expenditure trailed economic growth, the increase mostly more NHS expenditures, as the public sector remains the main source of health funding in all OECD countries, safe the U.S., and Mexico, that of 86% health spending in the U.K in 2004, versus 80% in 1998, and the 73% OECD average4. Incidentally, the U.S, 45%, and Mexico, 46% spent the least share of public funds on health in 2004 compared to other OECD countries, Japan, and Nordic countries such as Denmark, Norway, and Sweden, some of the highest. With the U.S for example, spending 15.3% of its GDP on health in 2004, by far, the most on health as a share of economy, worldwide, and projected to increase, the healthcare delivery issues countries face must have local flavors, but nonetheless, highlight the need for efforts geared toward realizing the dual healthcare delivery objectives mentioned earlier. In other words, the need for action is universal in health systems, as many of the problems albeit rooted in variegated institutional and jurisdictional issues, require solutions that tailgate toward achieving these dual healthcare objectives. This suggests the need for each locale to conduct a decomposition/exposition exercise of its peculiar healthcare delivery issues and problems, which would reveal the underlying issues and processes for which specific actions need initiated the process cycle analyses that result also revealing, barring any psychological fallacy, the appropriate healthcare ICT that would lead to the resolution of these issues. These technologies would also result in the modification of the processes to improve the outcome, healthcare delivery, and indeed, the achievement of the healthcare delivery objectives for the health jurisdiction. In the U.K for example, the number of acute care hospital beds was 3.6 per 1 000 population in 2004, the OECD average, 4.1 beds, a steady reduction in many of these countries in the past decade in tandem with a fall in the average length of hospital stays, and a rise in the number of same-day (or ambulatory) surgeries. Are these actions reminiscent of historical ad-hoc hospital closures or symptomatic of the changing face of healthcare delivery predicated on contemporary realities?

Some might ask why the resource limitations that have characterized the status quo for long have suddenly now taken on a new toga, literally, threatening to erase the gains of socialized welfare for example, toppling governments that have held sway in some cases for generations. This was the case recently in Sweden where the ruling Social Democratic Party lost the general elections and its 12-year hold on power in mid -September 2006, despite its pledge to reform social welfare in the country-reform social welfare in Sweden did you say? Merely suggesting this would have been anathema until now, in a country whose welfare system other countries endeavour to emulate, and where a right leaning party last won elections in 1979, a center-right coalition majority in the 349-member parliament by just one seat, not to mention one now winning that could essentially dismantle the famed welfare system. Should a country such as the U.S., in 2004 way ahead of other OECD countries on total health spending per capita, $US 6,100 (adjusted for purchasing power parity), over twice the US$2,550 OECD average and 15.3% of its GDP the highest among OECD countries, six percentage points more than the 8.9% average, and rising bother about curtailing health spending5? What if public funds account for only 45% of health spending, well below the 73% OECD average, in fact the lowest among OECD countries, private insurance, 37% of total health spending5, more than even others with relatively large shares of total health sp ending, over 12%, paid by private insurance such as Canada, France and the Netherlands? What if premiums for employer-sponsored health coverage increased 7.7% in 2006, averagely, albeit less than the 2005 9.2% and the 2003 13.9% increase and peak, respectively, premiums still up twice more than workers wages and overall inflation in 2005 premiums having increased 87%, wages, 20%, and inflation, 18% since 20006? Would these figures from the 2006 Employer Health Benefits Survey released on September 26, 2006, help us reconcile the angst the virtue it would tend to inspire in acting to forestall the tendency toward so many of us lacking access to qualitative healthcare being nonetheless antithetical to the Moorean moral/ natural disjunction with which we might struggle, our Kantian atavism? The Kaiser/HRET annual survey also showed enrolment in consumer-driven health plans to be modest. Is this evidence also of the flux in our conceptualizations of the action, another tension between to take which or not to, and how, if we did settle to act? Does the Kaiser Foundation s President and CEO Dr. Drew E. Altman, not put it succinctly that, While premiums didn't rise as fast as they have in recent years, working people don t feel like they are getting any relief at all because their premiums have been rising so much faster than their paycheques. Indeed, As he added, To working people and business owners a reduction in an already very high rate of increase just means you re still paying more. Should our action were w e to promote the consumer-driven healthcare delivery model more forcefully not involve revisiting the issues involved in its varied forms, reimbursement of healthcare professionals, regulatory/legislative measures, and tax/incentives measures, among others? What role would such an exercise play in relieving as HRET President, Dr. Mary A. Pittman put it, The burden of a fragmented system of coverage (that) falls heaviest on the small employer and their workers (With) about two in five small businesses do not even offer health insurance, and those that do require workers on average to contribute significantly more to their premiums for family coverage? What role would the deployment of the appropriate healthcare information and communication technologies, p lay in integrating the noted fragmentation in the country s health systems, and in the various issues and processes that would make the consumer-driven healthcare-delivery model work? No doubt, we recognize with increasing candour the ills of our health systems although it is uncertain that we really want to act on them, as it would appear we could with evidence palpable of the zeal, with which we approach the issues, and processes local to our health jurisdiction, and our methodologies in so doing. Thus, how could we expect to solve the problems that confront say the decision process to situate a CT-scanner in a town A s hospital with patronage X, next to another, B that has one with patronage Y, the latter ten times more, if we did not consider the annual running/maintenance costs of the scanner in town A? How would we, not considering what other required services these costs could offset, or the credentialing issues that might result in contracting experts, in town B, which its neighbour lacks, would encounter practicing across the state/provincial border in town A? Could we not also consider it better to develop service/product offerings in keeping with the available expertise in the hospital in town A, whose patronage by that in town B, and its peoples might just be what would make the hospital in town A remain financially viable hence not eventually moribund? These questions underscore the complexity of the decision making process in contemporary healthcare delivery, and the potential for the issues involved to engender new healthcare delivery ideas and models. They also bring into focus supplementary issues and processes, the resolution of all that would create additional delivery models, based on the emergence of newer issues and processes, which would be subject to modifications, the processes repeated ad infinitum. As this process cycle analyses would reveal, the appropriate healthcare ICT that would be invaluable in effecting such modifications, the eventual results, the realization of the dual healthcare delivery goals, should we not in fact support such modifications and their antecedents? To be sure, the issues are typically more far-reaching than offering support and require the concerted efforts of a variety of persons and organizations in equally disparate domains. This is why the recent withdrawal by Accenture from its role as the lead IT contractor for the NHS in the north-east and east regions of the UK, hence to services worth over £2billion is cause for concern7. Accenture has a hundred days to hand over responsibility to Computer Sciences Corporation (CSC) for all its ICT projects besides Picture Archiving and Communication Systems. This departure, for which Accenture stands finable, is no doubt symptomatic of the problems that have plagued the well-intentioned NHS IT program, including marked delays in project completion, although the progress the firm has made installing systems in the project is more than any other lead IT contractor7. In the deal made on September 29, 2006, CSC will receive £1965 million for nine years service to both regions, plus its supplies in the north-west and west to the NHS. This thrusts most of the £12.4bn national program on one IT firm, CSC, simultaneously increasing the pressure on its subcontractor iSoft, which m any would argue has enough of its own problems with which to contend. In particular, Accenture is blaming the software firm, on contract to provide software for three out of the five NHS IT regional hubs, for delays to critical frontline packages for examp le, Lorenzo. In fact, along with CSC, it is essentially questioning iSoft s project management and software development competence, even slamming it with a red alert in August 2006, regarding clinical safety, in response to which iSoft brought in a clinical safety expert although still uncertain on project completion date. This is not surprising, given a £344m pre-tax loss and scrutiny from the Financial Services Authority, the firm no doubt in dire financial straits. Richard Bacon, Tory MP, and John Pugh, Liberal Democrat MP, attributed the problems of the National Programme for IT (NPfIT), some of whose projects are two years behind schedule, in the main to over-centralization and over-ambition . According to the MP, The fundamental error made when setting up the program was to assume that centralized procurement of single systems across the NHS would be more efficient than local decision-making guided by national standards The project should be reformed so that local hospital Trusts can purchase locally systems which link into the national framework. These issues highlight the complexity of the actions that might need taken to expedite the achievement of the dual healthcare delivery goals, and that these actions are typically multifaceted, involving the collaboration among a variety of players. This in turn underscores a crucial point we have attempted to stress thus far, that of the need for literally going back to the basics, to have proper formulations of the underlying issues at the conceptual level, prior to moving on to the next stage, which is to engage in thorough process cycle analyses of the issues. This stage would reveal the sub-issues and processes, what we need to do to improve them, including the healthcare ICT we need to implement to do so. However, as we have seen in the example above, even the decomposition/exposition of these issues and processes, and the subsequent determination of healthcare ICT that we need to implement to improve them do not translate into the realization of the stated dual healthcare delivery goals. In particular, they would not without duly subjecting the issues and processes of the vendors and contractors that would implement the technologies, which we expect would improve the identified-processes that would result in the achievement of the goals to the same methodological rigor. Would it not be easier for these vendors and contractors to be on the same page literally with the rest of the healthcare stakeholders on the conceptual foundations of the projects on which they would embark? Would doing so not ensure that they embrace the thoroughness in preparation, and objectivity in approach crucial to executing successfully such major projects on which the lives of millions depend?

Some might wonder why vendors and contractors should concern themselves with the conceptual roots of healthcare delivery models. However cryptic the reasons are, in fact, they are not considering the economic implications of the project delays first for iSoft, and now for Accenture, not to mention image and goodwill-related ones. In fact, in an announcement of its full-year results in New York on September 29, 2006, Accenture noted that the NHS matter led to a fall in net revenues in the fourth quarter of $339m (£181m). Putting the political fallouts of these project delays in the picture, not to mention those negative opinions they engendered among the public no doubt complicates the situation for these firms further. This is notwithstanding that, the National Audit Office recently backed the four main IT contractors of NPfIT for achieving substantial progress , which some have in fact, dubbed a travesty , allegations of failures cover-ups by the watchdog. To be sure, Accenture made some progress having installed systems in 19 of the 20 work areas in its service of two-and-half-years versus 10, 5, and 3 areas for BT, CSC, and Fujitsu, respectively. Nonetheless, Tory health minister Stephen O'Brien on September 29, 2006 queried the government s conduct of the £6bn IT refit, calling on the National Audit Office needs to revisit the program . That Accenture could opt to cut its losses some would contend undermines the integrity of the entire program, and the minister observed, The government s failure to ensure that its Connecting for Health programme consulted widely enough and fully engaged users in the design and implementation has led to serious disillusionment amongst frontline NHS professionals. By failing to deliver quickly, the cost of the lost opportunity to improve patient care is rising dramatically. There is also the symbiotic relationship between progress in healthcare delivery and in healthcare information and communications technologies, one feeding into the other, creating opportunities for both that neither could ignore. Nor could they also that of the overall health of a nation on its economic productivity, hence growth and sustainable development. With regard the former for example, there is no doubt about the wisdom in health systems embracing the population health approach to health and healthcare delivery issues, developing programs aimed at primary, secondary, and tertiary prevention for example. There is also none for example about the immense benefits of preventing diseases from occurring in the first place, primary prevention, in fact, preempting them, which latter, research in genomics, proteonomics, and related fields would help us achieve, essentially identifying aberrant genomic profiles that could result in even hitherto-unknown diseases. Diagnosing and treating diseases promptly, which is secondary prevention also would certainly reduce morbidities and mortalities, improving the quality of healthcare delivery and saving healthcare costs substantially. Tertiary prevention, which essentially involves putting the necessary structures and programs in place, including rehabilitation programs, for the prevention of the long-term sequelae of diseases, and their effective treatments, is also doubtless an important element of our quest to achieve the dual healthcare delivery goals. Would the development of innovative programs in these three areas not inspire creativity in healthcare information technologies with potentially significant market potential? Would such programs not emerge with the appropriate healthcare stakeholders, doctors, lab technicians, social workers, community health nurses, primary care physicians, and managers, for example, engaging in a thorough process cycle analysis of their respective domains, working alone or collaborating with related domains, their IT departments, and even external consultants and vendors? Take the wait times issue. It is a key healthcare-access issue that healthcare jurisdictions worldwide need to address, that is to reduce wait times, and one spawning a generation of healthcare ICT solutions, for example that by Computer Sciences Corporation (CSC). The firm recently announced that implementing its Patient Administration System in Greater Manchester, reduced how long it takes to register new referrals at The North Manchester Primary Care NHS Trust (PCT) podiatry clinic8, from up to ten weeks to averagely three. This is a remarkable reduction, more so for a department operated on a self-referral basis, open to any resident of the North Manchester Primary Care NHS Trust (PCT) with a podiatry need. According to Helene Gordon, Deputy Head of Podiatry at the clinic, The system appears to be bringing some benefits to our patients not only have waiting times dropped dramatically, but patients are now able to choose dates and times that are suitable for them, which means we have fewer missed appointments. How does the system work? Patients contact the local clinic, fill in an application form, a clerk sends the paperwork to the podiatry department via internal mail, the details then logged on the computer, the paper work sent back to the original clinic, again via internal mail. Clinics then post to the patient, the next available appointment, who then attends or does not. As Martin Lomax, Account Executive Greater Manchester from The CSC Alliance noted, The introduction of the computerized system along with business change management has allowed the department to miss out a number of the steps that were previously required in the appointment process which has resulted in the fundamental increase in level of service offered to patients. This means that the system has become more efficient, with which comes costs savings, overall gains in the efficiency and effectiveness of care delivery, with costs savings as a bonus, essentially, the elements of the dual healthcare delivery objectives. Consider also if should it not inspire technological innovation for doctor/doctor information sharing that might save someone s life that suffers from a rare genetic disorder that results in lethal toxin accumulating in the bloodstream, who going into coma, on arrival at the ER, the spouse could not convince the doctor to give the agent needed to reduce the toxin. The ER doctor did not believe the spouse, spent precious time trying to contact the patient s GP, on the phone, to no avail, the patient dead a while later. How many more patients die daily or their illnesses unduly prolonged due to such communication lack/delays depriving doctors of the critical information that they need often in real time to manage their patients conditions more efficiently and effectively? To think that unlike other similarly information-intensive industries such as the banking and insurance industries are ahead of the health industry in the utilization of information and communication technologies by at least a decade according to some estimates is simply perplexing, although probably true. Should we not be preventing unnecessary morbidities and mortalities developing the right healthcare ICT that would make complete and accurate patient information available promptly, and in real time at the point of care (POC)? Should we not be decomposing/exposing the complex business, technical, regulatory, financial, political, sociological, and whatever issues in the way in achieving this goal, and would such exercises not be spawning innovative healthcare ICT that would facilitate their resolution? Does process analyzing the process of the developers of these technologies not ring true in this regard? With as many as 98000 deaths occurring every year in the U.S., alone due to medical errors according to a widely-quoted the Institute of Medicine report, To Err Is Human: Building a Safer Health System, and 1.5 million people experience adverse drug interactions, mistaken doses, and a variety of other medication errors, we indeed, need such analyses. We need the technologies that would provide physicians patient information at the POC for example, or enable e-prescribing, or computerized physician order entry, among others, that would help prevent medication errors, and save lives, and these needs continue to motivate the creation of such technologies. Thus, an all-inclusive system of electronic health records (EHR) that connect healthcare providers, hospitals, insurance firms, and other healthcare stakeholders in the U.S, providing POC access to patient information, its national Health Information Network (NHIN) would likely be operational fully by 2014. Other countries, such as the U.K, whose NPfIT program we mentioned earlier, Canada, via the Canada Health Infoway, Australia, Canada, Finland, Germany, and Denmark, to mention a few are also embarking on a similar project to automate medical records, Finland in fact probably going to launch its interoperable patient records in late 2006, and Canada, in 2010. However, the problems of NPfIT, mentioned above are potential obstacles to bear in mind regarding the efforts of these other countries. Interestingly, the NHIN is principally private sector inspired although with federal support/funding, and will have a centralized system and many independently managed regional networks, akin to the Internet. Doctors will have a longitudinal view of their patients medical histories, facilitating the institution of innovative primary preventive programs, and not just those aimed at secondary, or even tertiary prevention, which highlights the point made earlier about the symbiosis between progress in healthcare delivery vis-à-vis in healthcare information and communication technologies. With U.S., healthcare costs soaring, up to US $1.9 trillion, or as noted earlier, more than 15% of the country s GDP, NHIN when operational, would no doubt help substantially curtail these costs, while also improving healthcare delivery, essentially in achieving the dual healthcare delivery goals. It would also over time, facilitate the conduct of research forexamples, public health studies and disease/bioterrorism surveillance, among others, the conduct of which would also stimulate the development of novel technologies in a continuous quality improvement process in both domains that would feed ceaselessly into each other. For this reason alone, and considering, as the examples given above show, the dividends in saved lives, and in the elimination and/or reduction in morbidities derivable from the healthcare delivery/healthcare ICT dyadic, doctors and other healthcare providers ought to change the essentially nonchalant attitude of the healthcare industry to healthcare ICT. As the industry s key leaders, and those responsible primarily, for the delivery of qualitative health services, this means that healthcare providers should embrace the technologies more than they do currently and not just implement but also utilize them in their daily practice.

Indeed, they should heed the call from various quarters, for example, that of President George W. Bush for the creation of nationwide health information system in his 2004 State of the Union addresses, and collaborate with their colleagues and other healthcare stakeholders to meet the president s set goal of creating electronic health records for most Americans by 2014. This is more so, as noted earlier that even if not immediately obvious, or taken notice office readily, the effect of the overall health of a nation on its economic productivity, hence growth and sustainable development is not in doubt. Thus by heeding these calls, healthcare providers are also contributing their quotas to their country's sustainable economic development. This reminds us of the problem posed earlier on regarding policy choices on health financing. For example it highlights how much costs burden we should place on people seeking healthcare with skyrocketing out-of-pocket expenditures, were we serious about equitable access to health services, and at what costs, not so doing to the entire populace, as the paradoxical increase in health spending that the ensuing overall poor health and poverty cycle occasion magnifies. How do we marry these with the need to fund health systems without compromise the national budget? Do these issues not warrant revisiting how we currently run our health systems to see if we could change anything that would solve our healthcare delivery conundrum? Considering the symbiotic relationship between healthcare delivery and healthcare inform ation and communication technologies mentioned earlier, could we not in a sense turbo-charge this dyadic hoping we could forge creative healthcare delivery models and their correspondingly innovative healthcare ICT to move the entire process of healthcare delivery forward and perhaps much quicker toward the accomplishment of the dual healthcare delivery objectives? With the average healthcare consumer becoming increasingly suave in his/her expectations of the health system and of healthcare delivery, the population in many countries, particularly the developed countries aging fast, and chronic diseases that guzzle medications and hospitalizations costs becoming more prevalent, there is certainly need for some form of action in the health sector to address these issues. Furthermore, with healthcare costs soaring, coupled with our quest mentioned above to resolve the pervasive inequities in healthcare access among different groups, the time for action is now, which makes unsurprising the focus of major bodies, for example, the OECD, on the issue of ensuring health systems financial sustainability, simultaneously, that they add something and positively to macroeconomic performance. In other words, health systems must operate on value-added propositions that justify their very survival on the one hand, yet they must deliver more qualitative health services, ensure universal and equitable access to health services. Do these not essentially make it imperative for health systems to seek to attain the dual healthcare delivery goals mentioned earlier? Since, again, as we mentioned earlier, there would always be local flavours to the requirements of peoples served by different health jurisdictions, even within the same country, does this not mean that each would have to seek ways relevant to these requirements in achieving these goals? Even in a health system with major public funding, there is no disputing the fact that health jurisdiction stands the chances of merging or closing down some of it health facilities that are no longer economically viable to run, and we have started to see in Quebec for example, a new pattern of hospital mergers. This is something that other healthcare jurisdiction in Canada, and indeed, elsewhere would no doubt consider in particular as they inevitably start to re- conceptualize health investments and the formulation of health financing policies. They would have to start doing these in terms a health/economy dyadic, of health parameters such as mortality, morbidity, and disability being reliant on living standards on the one hand, but also on the health systems quality and performance, which means formulating policies that could improve both, and not just either of these domains. They would no longer be able to dismiss offhand, the profound effects of health on their countries overall economy, and would need to strive to synchronize health and economic policies to improve their chances to be able to achieve the dual healthcare delivery goals. There is no doubt therefore, that all healthcare stakeholders have something indeed, at stake in ensuring the achievement of these dual healthcare delivery goals. This is because we all would go down with the economy literally, the healthcare provider, the small and big business operators, the policy makers, all of us, if we did nothing to stop or failed to contribute to ensuring the health system does not sink. It is therefore necessary for all of us to participate some way in the process cycle analyses mentioned above in our various domains, health, or non-health, as our contribution in this regard would add in no small measure to the overall efforts of determining the obstacles to the smooth and efficient running of our health systems. It is clear therefore that the varieties of these analyses are legion, ranging from the few steps in the processes of an office clerk in the entirety of the scheme of things, that is the overall healthcare delivery processes, to the most complex processes that some other actor in the scheme might have to deal with. The crucial thing is to identify the issues at stake and to decompose them into sub-issues, which perhaps would involve the operations of different units and different departments, which again, underscores the need for collaboration with colleagues at different levels, the potential for exposition, much higher this way. The emphasis on this analytic process underlines the necessity for the sort of thorough understanding of the different levels of the domains relevant to the outcome of the exercises, healthcare delivery, qualitatively, and cost-effectively, that would reveal the needs for and the appropriate healthcare information and communication technologies required to improve the processes underlying healthcare delivery. Considering the pivotal roles of doctors and other healthcare providers in healthcare delivery and the significance of the success of these roles in not just in improving the health of their clients, their quest for professional fulfillment, and in the achievement of the dual healthcare delivery goals, among others, doctors cannot afford to be mute about their healthcare ICT needs. They also need to be active participants in the processes that could call for massive changes in their practices and the healthcare delivery models involved with them. Incidentally, these changing models would also likely influence their remuneration schemes, for example, what changes would the increasing use of electronic consultations, via e-mail, text messages, even bidirectional video-consultation such as via a simple webcam that is becoming increasingly ubiquitous at least in the developed world, mean for how the doctors involved receive payment for their services? Would insurers be willing to pay for such services, which by the way could be important even life saving under certain circumstances, such as the prompt SMS message to the teenage female on the outcome of a high vaginal swab that showed an infection, including directives on treatment, perhaps to pick the antibiotics up at the nearest pharmacy. Consider the benefits to that teenager that would not materialize were delay in treating the infection likely to compromise her reproductive future, possibly even survival, the SMS message not sent, and the teenager not reached otherwise, because for example, she was not in town, and no one knew where she was. These are examples, and there are many more of novel technologies spawning treatment paradigms and vice versa, but not the appropriate response from the other players in the healthcare delivery process, for example insurance firms. These are issues, again, many more also exist, for example, in some instances, relating to credentialing, that require the collaboration between doctors, and the other parties involved rather jettison a potentially valuable technological resource. By not participating actively in such matters, doctors and healthcare professionals are not just denying their patients the benefits accruable from modern and continually evolving healthcare information and communication technologies, but interru pting the supposedly equally perpetual symbiotic dyadic between healthcare delivery and these technologies. This, even if they cared less about the latter, still translates into stalling the progress of their very own profession. Indeed, not just that, as it also means creating, albeit unwittingly, the enabling milieu for the perpetuation of all the problems attributable to defective healthcare delivery including, as several IOM reports, including the one mentioned earlier concerning the thousands of needless deaths due to medical errors. Since it is unlikely that any doctor would set out to do such things, doctors need also not expose their profession to charges of errors of omission. This is why they need to be proactive regarding issues pertaining to the widespread adoption and utilization of healthcare information and communication technologies among their ranks, and indeed, in the health industry at large.

New healthcare delivery models would of necessity, emerge in different countries, and in different health jurisdictions within the same country. We should expect this to happen considering our discussion thus far on the peculiarities of the requirements of health jurisdiction based on a variety of socio-demographic, health, economic, political, institutional, and other factors, including the state of development of technological infrastructure in the health jurisdiction. However, there are obstacles in the way, in particular in the sense of the blockage or lack of interest in promoting the adoption of healthcare ICT could inhibit the emergence of such novel and potentially valuable healthcare delivery models. A case in point is the chances of a healthcare IT bill reaching Congress for a vote before fall recess started on September 29, 2006, in the U.S., although some contend that it still could pass during a lame duck session expected to start Nov. 13 200610. The underpinning of such a law is that it could save lives and contain costs by eliminating duplication of medical testing, noted Justin T. Barnes, vice president of marketing and government affairs at Greenway Medical Technology, who thrice testified before Congress on healthcare IT and assisted on the language for the proposed law. Barnes also noted the inability of Congress to reconcile language between House bill 4157, the Health Information Technology Promotion Act, lacking language on interoperability and Senate bill 1418, the Wired for Healthcare Quality Act. To underscore the different directions from which the bill is receiving knocks, Dr. Deborah C. Peel, founder of the Patient Privacy Rights Foundation, contended that passing a healthcare IT law without proper patient privacy protection in place, which the current bill seems to lack, would no doubt be problematic. She noted, It is unconscionable that leadership is not paying attention to the stories of how vulnerable our medical records are Information doesn't stay where consumers want it to stay The more time we have for the American public to realize the potential dangers, the better. Meantime, Barnes on the other hand affirmed the determination he and others have to get the bill passed, stressing, We will definitely crank this back up again next year with a better bill and we will have a more educated congress to work with. He added, If need be, the IT bill will be re-crafted into several smaller bills, ensuring better odds of getting them passed. Here again we see the need for process analyzing issues regardless of the domain concerned that pertain to the realization of the outcome of the healthcare delivery efforts, exemplified in both the concerns of Dr Peel, and the intended approach of Mr. Barnes. It is clear from this example, and we see that a doctor is indeed involved, the need for physicians to be active participants in health care ICT issues. There is no doubt that rather than being opposed to the passage of the bill for its own sake or for some other reasons inimical to the progress of her profession she actually wants the bill to include the necessary provisions that would do the exact opposite. The fact that concerns by the public regarding the privacy and confidentiality of personal health information during electronic communication and sharing by healthcare professionals has been a major obstacle to the widespread diffusion of healthcare ICT is no secret, which explains Dr Peel s stand on the bill. In other words, it explains the chances that if passed without such provisions the bill would likely even worsen the prospects of these technologies gaining wider currency, which might be why Mr. Barnes wants to decompose it further, again, and either way, testament to the complexities of the interplay of issues that would drive healthcare delivery in future. It also underlines why doctors, the team leaders essentially in the healthcare delivery process, cannot afford to lag behind on these issues. Another such critical issue to progress in healthcare delivery, and which doctors cannot afford to shun is that of assuring the quality of healthcare delivery. Indeed, this issue is central to our discussion thus far, as it ties firmly with the need for health systems to achieve the dual healthcare delivery objectives we have stressed so much. In the U.S., the Centers for Medicare and Medicaid Services (CMS) recently announced an update to its Hospital Quality Alliance Web site, adding to the site data on heart attack and failure, pneumonia, and surgical infection prevention data from hospitals through 200511, part of ongoing quality initiative efforts announced in several areas in recent w eeks. Indeed, HHS Secretary Leavitt has affirmed that quality measurement is his first priority, even suggested that quality measurement be tied to the implementation of health information exchange (HIE) as various states implement their HIE projects12. In late September 2006, the Institute of Medicine issued the report Rewarding Provider Performance: Aligning Incentives in Medicare that emphasized the need for inducements for healthcare provider participation in quality reporting and that of phasing in implementation within a learning system13. Other recent quality-related developments include the initiation by the AQA-HQA Steering Committee of new work groups to investigate quality measure harmonization, cost-pricing transparency, and other issues relating to pilots ongoing across the U.S., Secretary Leavitt planning to meet with the pilots to determine coupling best practices with quality efforts around the country. He also intends to meet with the key 100 employers in the country to emphasize the need for standardized quality measures and transparency14. Clearly, the commitment of the U.S. health authorities to quality is strong, and understandably so, considering the country s equally firm intention to reduce its soaring healthcare costs while simultaneously ensuring the delivery of high quality healthcare to its peoples. Part of ensuring quality is accountability and transparency, which again, is paramount on the minds of U.S. authorities, as the new work plan the Office of Inspector General (OIG) recently posted for fiscal year 2007 shows15. The work plan highlighted various projects the Office of Audit Services, Office of Evaluation and Inspections, Office of Investigations, and Office of Counsel to the Inspector General would undertake during the fiscal year. Among them are payments for observation services versus inpatient admission for dialysis services; inpatient hospital payments for new technology; outpatient department payments; unbundling of hospital outpatient services; and medical appropriateness and coding of DRG services. Others are review of evaluation and management services during global surgery periods; inpatient rehabilitation-facility compliance with Medicare requirements; long-term care hospital payments; accurately coding claims for Medicare home-health resource groups; and skilled nursing facility consolidated billing15. With the Why Not the Best? Results of the Commonwealth Fund Commission on a High Performance Health System , which has established the National Scorecard on US Health System Performance to measure and monitor healthcare outcomes, quality, access, efficiency, and equity not quite impressive, should the authorities not bother?16 The Why Not the Best? Results from a National Scorecard on US Health System Performance that analyzes the scorecard and the US healthcare system s results showed that on 37 indicators, the US health system scored an average of 66% comparing actual national performance to achievable standard s. That scores on efficiency were very low attests to the need for process improvement within the health system, which implementing the appropriate healthcare ICT, determined by the sort of process cycle analyses we have stressed in our discussion, could help achieve. The scorecard evaluates how well the US health system is performing in general, relative to what it could achieve the scores arrived at from ratios weighing the country s national average performance to benchmarks, representing top performance. Again, these scores indicate the need for improvement in healthcare delivery in the country, which itself explains its soaring health spending, as one would expect with the corresponding increase in morbidities and mortalities that defective healthcare delivery would eventually engender. That the U.S. is taking measures to address this problem is no doubt the appropriate thing to do, and its example should instruct other countries both in the developed and developing world of the need for action to tackle their healthcare delivery problems with as much vigor as they could. This also means the need for full cooperation of the doctors and other healthcare providers in the exercise, including regarding adopting a more positive outlook to the potential role that healthcare ICT could play in their health systems successfully overcoming the challenges they face. Indeed, these examples highlight the multidimensional nature of the issues and processes that coalesce into the outcome we term healthcare delivery and why any genuine intention to improve it, would necessarily involve process analyzing these issues. Such analyses need not be en bloc, which in fact is impracticable if not impossible, but require each domain, including of doctors and other healthcare providers, individually and in tandem with others decomposing and exposing relevant issues and processes. The examples also point to the potential for healthcare ICT to improve healthcare delivery, by improving issues via their processes in the different domains, health, and nonhealth alike that contribute to the realization of healthcare delivery, in fact also modifying it, new models of care emerging in the process.

We have focused on the effect of the dyadic between healthcare delivery and healthcare ICT in spawning new healthcare delivery models, which is an added albeit inevitable benefit to our efforts at continuous improvement in the quality of healthcare delivery, which itself would foster the achievement of another key healthcare delivery objective that of curtailing health costs. In other words, by simply em bracing healthcare ICT and exploring how they could help us improve processes underlying germane healthcare issues, via a thorough decomposition/exposition process cycle analysis, we create the opportunities for our health systems to move increasingly closer to the necessarily elusive destination of perfection. Thus, we accept that our health systems could never be perfect, not least as we cannot, not perhaps until we could preempt diseases, determine when a new bug with the potential to create a new disease with an entirely novel transmission, and clinical pattern, would emerge, and torpedo the status quo of our health system, necessitating dramatic changes to it. Doctors have a major role to play in this exercise as key players in the healthcare delivery, which explains why they need to improve on the implications of such findings as the results of a recent study from the Center for Studying Health System Change (HSC17.) In 2004/05 according to the study, only about one in four physicians (24%) use e-mail in their practice to communicate clinical issues with patients and most use physician-patient e-mail. Physicians in staff/group-model HMOs and medical school faculty practices use e-mail the most, followed by doctors in group practices with over 50 physicians, only about 20% of doctors in practices with nine or less doctors, essentially the smaller practices, using the technology. The study also noted that although some patients are keen to communicate with their doctors via e-mail, not all patients have access to e-mail in particular, those living in rural areas, and low -income, elderly, and African-American healthcare consumers, less likely to have Internet access and even if they did, use e-mail17. At a time when the email is, becoming an increasingly potent technology, as the decision of Yahoo, reported on September 29, 2006, to enlist independent programmers in creating new services using its popular consumer e-mail program, shows, and considering the potential of this technology is facilitating healthcare delivery, more doctors and other healthcare professionals should in fact be using it18. Yahoo officials said that the firm plans to give away the underlying code to Yahoo Mail to encourage software developers to develop new applications based on e-mail, which creates an opening for software developers in the health sector to come up with innovative ideas for the application of this technology in healthcare delivery. This would be in keeping with progress with the symbiotic dynamics of the healthcare ICT and healthcare delivery dyadic mentioned earlier. In fact, the decision to open up the code of Yahoo Mail, which almost 300 million individuals use worldwide, anticipates stimulating interests in building thousands of new e-mail applications by both Yahoo engineers and those on their own, and in outside firms. The open approach to programming is perhaps the largest single Web software ever opened up for public development. Software developers have customarily kept such codes secret, only allowing outsiders to make only incremental updates on them, but times are changing as software firms realize that opening up these codes inspire novel and creative programming. Developers are thus able to merge software features from disparate firms to forge hybrid web products termed mashups , as happened with open applications such as Yahoo s Flickr and Google Maps. In technical terms, Yahoo is giving gratis browser-based authentication for its e-mail service, access to which code only Yahoo Mail and a few broadband associates such as AT&T and BT have. The access would enable individuals with the expertise to customize e-mails basic interface, or look, or others such as developing new information display means, among others, using the information in a user s e-mail program, with no risk of security breaches as Yahoo maintains absolute control of usernames and passwords. These opportunities for outside development would no doubt improve the efficiency and effectiveness of the e-mail program, making it even more versatile, which applied to healthcare delivery would certainly be a bonus, and one that could open up new ways of delivering qualitative health services. Indeed, to underscore the significance of this development, that is opening up the underlying code of Yahoo s em ail program other firms are suit for examples key Internet firms such as Amazon.com, Google, and eBay and software firms for examples Microsoft and IBM. The code, which would be out in late 2006, would likely inspire other e-mail providers to open up their programs codes, fostering the development of a mashup that allows users to simultaneously read Yahoo Mail, Google s Gmail and Microsoft s Hotmail from the same browser window for example, users not having to sign into each e-mail system individually. The potential for innovation that this move could generate is immense, and could benefit the health sector significantly, hence the need for more usage in doctor/patient communication. The email is just one among a variety of healthcare information and comm unication technologies that could be useful in healthcare delivery, the range too wide to catalogue here. Suffice to say that these technologies point the way forward for innovation in healthcare delivery including the development of new models of care. As we have noted all along, and as the example of the email given above shows, we stand a better chance of maximizing the potential benefits of the technologies for the improvement of healthcare delivery and the realization of the dual healthcare delivery goals, the more widespread their deployment in the various domains that result in healthcare delivery. Doctors have a major role in spearheading this widespread adoption of healthcare ICT, a role thrust upon them at the very least by the very nature of the commitment that they swore to do no harm to their patients implies. In doing no harm, they should intuitively be doing good as far as, some would argue, we could ascribe graspable reasons to the choices we make regarding our actions in realizing it, our choices, and the reasons for them evident of our values hence we are what we do. In this sense, not acting to prevent the large-scale disease burden that could result from a defective health system would therefore equally represent our values, for example, not embracing the healthcare ICT that could help prevent/rectify the defect. Yet, even doctors are human, and are not lacking in virtue, their determination to act even if they had to go the extra mile, literally, to ensure that their patients and fellow humans do not languish in disease and poverty capable of emerging from within, independently and freely.

References

1. Available at: http://www.washingtonpost.com/wp-

dyn/content/article/2006/09/26/AR2006092600768.html Accessed on September 28, 2006

2. Available at: http://www.kff.org/insurance/7527/index.cfm Accessed on September 29, 2006

3. Available at: http://www.hm-

treasury.gov.uk/Spending_Review/spend_sr02/report/spend_sr02_repchap07.cf m Accessed on September 29, 2006

4. Available at:

http://www.oecd.org/country/0,3021,en_33873108_33873870_1_1_1_1_1,00.html Accessed on September 29, 2006

5. Available at:

http://www.oecd.org/country/0,3021,en_33873108_33873886_1_1_1_1_1,00.html Accessed on September 29, 2006

6. Available at: http://www.kff.org/insurance/ehbs092606nr.cfm Accessed on September 29, 2006

7. Available at: http://www.contractoruk.com/news/002874.html Accessed on September 30, 2006

8. Available at: http://uk.country.csc.com/en/ne/pr/5445.shtml Accessed on September 30, 2006

9. Available at: http://www.iom.edu/CMS/8089/5575/4117.aspx Accessed on September 30, 2006

10. Available at: http://www.healthcareitnews.com/printStory.cms?id=5629 Accessed on September 30, 2006

11. Available at: http://www.hospitalcompare.hhs.gov/ Accessed on October 1, 2006

12. Available at: http://www.hhs.gov/healthit/ahic.html Accessed on October 1, 2006

13. Available at: http://www.nap.edu Accessed on October 1, 2006

14. Available at: http://www.nap.edu. Accessed on October 1, 2006

15. Available at: http://tinyurl.com/hobr8 Accessed on October 1, 2006

16. Available at: http://www.cmwf.org/publications/publications

_show.htm?doc_id=401577. Accessed on October 1, 2006

17. Available at: http://www.hschange.org. Accessed on October 1, 2006

18. Available at: http://news.com.com/2102-1032_3-6121552.html?tag=st.util.print Accessed on October 1, 2006

Conclusion

The weight of research evidence no doubt suggests the immense benefits of healthcare information and communication technologies to healthcare delivery. There is also no doubt that more doctors are starting to embrace these technologies, but the pace as we have seen throughout this book is still painfully slow. This is certainly cause for concern considering that we cannot expect patients that need these technologies to improve their health, perhaps even to save their lives to wait until doctors make their minds up to implement and use these valuable technologies. This is the core reason we have embarked on the journey together to discuss the relevant issues regarding this matter in this book. We would at least have succeeded in one thing doing so, that is, raising the awareness of doctors and other healthcare stakeholders on the issues germane to the interface of healthcare delivery and healthcare information and communication technologies, and indeed, as we surmised, to the symbiotic dyadic these two domains constitute. Besides the role these technologies play in helping us achieve the dual healthcare delivery objectives that we mentioned so often in this book, they also feed into the healthcare delivery processes to stimulate the emergence of novel healthcare-delivery models. These models in turn feed back into the healthcare ICT domain to inspire the development of even new er technologies that would further improve healthcare delivery. There is no doubt, therefore regarding the scope of the contributions that doctors would be making adopting these technologies on a wider scale.

With the potential for the outbreak of novel viruses, and other bugs, and indeed, of the onset of a variety of other disruptive processes, manmade or natural, not to mention the inherent evolutionary tendency of any system that mere randomness could instigate and direct, our health systems being subject to change, planned and unplanned, could never be perfect. Given this state of affairs, should we not consider it a privilege that we have such a self-motorized symbiotic dyadic? Why should all we need to do, which is to implement these technologies therefore be such a chore? Granted that we do not just go shopping for them, and that we need to engage in thorough analyses of the issues involved in the realization of healthcare delivery, what we termed the process cycle analysis, should that not in fact be an exercise we should conduct on an ongoing basis as part of our quality improvement efforts? The point here is that without constantly deciphering the imperfections in our health systems via such process cycle analyses, its defect would progressively magnify, the system eventually slowly stopping. Now, no one would say that this is a desirable state of affairs, considering the economic costs and the disease burden on individuals and society as a whole of such a situation. Yet, the experience of many health systems worldwide is akin to this slow progression towards imminent demise. These issues clearly demand our urgent attention, which explains the logic in our discussion in this book regarding doctors and their attitudes toward healthcare information and communication technologies, for obvious reasons, they being the primary proponents of healthcare delivery. As we noted earlier, the direction of the forces driving contemporary healthcare delivery is toward doctors having to reconsider their views on these technologies and to see them as integral if not critical components of their practice even now, but more so in the years ahead.

We must keep our vision of healthcare delivery in focus, and continue to provide the healthcare consumer the best health services that we could, given our peculiar circumstances. Again as evident in our discussions, the issues that concern healthcare delivery would vary by health jurisdiction, even within the same country, which underscores the need for each to conduct process cycle analysis that would reveal the appropriate solutions to its problems. Healthcare delivery is a very complex phenomenon, with components that are clinical and non-clinical, both domains nonetheless working in tandem, and necessarily so, toward the outcome we term healthcare delivery. Thus, our consideration of the applications of healthcare information and communication technologies in healthcare delivery should not focus on just one of these domains, hence doctors not having anything to do with the issues in the non-clinical domain, or the hospital manager, with those in the clinical, is out of the question. What we have seen in our discussion in this book is that on the contrary, developments in one domain could literally cripple activities in the other. It is this sort of broad -based multidimensional mindset toward what healthcare delivery is all about that would indeed, save our health systems from total annihilation by the economic, social, political, and other forces impinging on it in our contemporary times, and indeed, in future. At the end of the day, healthcare delivery is about people, about patient care, about preventing disease, and about promoting health, which clearly indicate the need to reach these peoples since they are not all in all location. Indeed, the more efficient we reach them, the better. These are fundamental principles that support the benefits of healthcare ICT that no doctor or anyone for that matter could deny. That we might not be deriving full benefits from these technologies as yet could be due to a variety of reasons including not enough doctors and other healthcare professionals implementing them, or deploying their full features. Healthcare technology vendors also need to embark on a continuous quality control and improvement exercise to make their products and services more relevant to healthcare needs in their chosen markets. This again underlines the point about process cycle analyses being required across board for us to achieve the desired dual healthcare delivery objectives.

Healthcare delivery has indeed become such an important element of our socio-economic milieu that no health jurisdiction could afford to ignore. There is no doubt that doctors recognize this fact, as even their practices would collapse were the health system so to do, albeit in the long term, as in fact, no country could sustain its economic productivity without a healthy and vibrant populace. Because of the global nature of our world, the economic consequences of diseases and poverty could transcend geographical, hence national boundaries. It is therefore in our collective interests to strive to provide everyone with qualitative healthcare in all countries around the world. Incidentally, and despite the differences in the stages of development of technological infrastructures and other institutions in different parts of the world, information communication and sharing still constitute critical elements of the achievement of the dual healthcare delivery goals. This calls for the need to bridge the so-called digital divide, which incidentally is not restricted to that between the rich and poor nations, as there are places even in the developed world that essentially lack the infrastructures for, hence access to healthcare ICT. Again, and as we have seen in our discussion, each jurisdiction would have to determine its healthcare ICT needs, no matter how minimal, which would still help, in its achievement of the dual healthcare delivery goals. Furthermore, doctors would have a major role to play in these efforts, regardless of the health jurisdiction in which they operate. As we highlight these various dimensions of the need for the use of healthcare information and communication technologies in healthcare delivery, it becomes increasingly clear the central role that these technologies would play in future healthcare delivery. Considering that they would be so crucial to healthcare delivery, should doctors not in fact begin to implement them en masse? In countries such as the United States, where there is a major private health insurance component to healthcare financing, would they not eventually need to do so for their practices to survive, let alone thrive?

In as much as we want to doctors to implement healthcare ICT, we need to encourage them to do so considering that these technologies are not often cheap, and typically require ongoing maintenance costs. Software vendors need to make their products affordable to as many doctors as possible for example, while both the public and private sectors should in fact initiate inducement programs to promote healthcare ICT among doctors. Doctors too need to realize that by attaining a critical mass implementing healthcare ICT, prices would have to fall as competition among vendors for patronage become fiercer, a situation that would also result in the latter becoming even more inventive in their value propositions to doctors and the health industry at large. This would doubtless augur well for the development of healthcare models, and in fact healthcare delivery overall, as we noted earlier. In short, the efforts of all stakeholders in promoting the widespread diffusion of healthcare information and communication technologies would bear fruit literally, in a variety of ways, all leading toward the achievement of the dual healthcare delivery objectives, on an enduring basis. These arguments point in the direction of the need for doctors to spearhead the healthcare ICT diffusion efforts, and close the gap between the vision of the provision of high quality and accessible health services to all and the reality on the ground in many countries worldwide. Their efforts in this regard would be beneficial in the short and the long terms to them, as professionals, in the fulfillment, they would experience in helping their patients in regaining their health and staying well, and in their health system, and indeed, their country in achieving the dual healthcare delivery goals.

Doctors are no doubt busy people. Asking them to implement and use healthcare information and communication technologies would be for some, a form of torture, in particular those that are not technologically inclined, as many of them tend to put it. There is therefore going to be the need for training in the basic applications that such doctors would perhaps at best implement, which nonetheless is a step in the right direction. It is possible that by starting to use these basic applications, they would become more at-ease with and proficient in the use of these and other technologies, and might implement even more technologies. As there might be quite a few such doctors, perhaps healthcare software and ICT vendors should consider marketing scaled -down versions of their products with less steep learning curves, but which would still essentially perform some asp ects of the overall features of the full-blown versions. On the other hand, some of the studies that have challenged the benefits of these technologies have indicated that the problems they noted in their studies might have been due to the doctors interviewed not having implemented the technologies in full, hence not deriving full benefits from them. This is why it is important to arrive at a viable compromise based on the peculiarities of both the software/ICT systems in question, and the market targeted. No doubt, the need to implement these technologies progressively would arise in some cases, due to either the major financial outlay involved, or the scope or complexities of the information systems in question, or indeed, any other reason. The important thing is to ensure that doctors, and other healthcare providers, continue to feel inclined to invest in these technologies, the return on investment (ROI) on which in many instances is not immediately obvious, the potential disinterest due to cost-escalating project delays, among others.

There is no doubt that health systems would continue to initiate whatever efforts would make them survive. This is going to task many of them to the point of fiscal exhaustion but it seems that, with the current level of awareness of the value of healthcare information and communication technologies in achieving the dual healthcare delivery goals, many would pull through. Furthermore, with continuing efforts by all concerned stakeholders to keep raising this awareness levels in their respective health jurisdictions and beyond, it would be much easier for health systems to comprehend their losses shunning healthcare ICT.

Doctors are going to need to lead these efforts and as we have noted over and over, it is not just in their interests to do so, they have ethico-moral obligations to meet regarding care provision to their patients that straddle the healthcare delivery/healthcare information and communication technologies interface. Our discussion in this book should form the fou ndation for more participation not just by doctors, and other healthcare professionals, but also other healthcare stakeholders in the concerted efforts to promote the implementation and use of healthcare information and communication technologies.

Governments need to start to see healthcare provision to their peoples not as costs but investments in human capital, albeit in the long term. This does not mean that they should jettison efforts to curtail soaring health spending and that they should not aim to provide high-quality health service simultaneously. On the contrary, they would likelier realize the dividends they expected to reap in their long term investments in health services ensuring that they pursue the achievement of these dual health care delivery goals with vigor. Health must receive the attention it deserves in any government s efforts at caring for its peoples. In other words, at the end of the day, regardless of the funding system of a country s health services, the role that government has to play in health service delivery is crucial, its nature and scope dependent however, on the particular country in question. Our discussion in this book has taken us through some of the key issues that influence contemporary healthcare delivery, and that would chart its future direction. There is no doubt that we have been able to demonstrate in many different ways the importance of healthcare information and communication technologies to healthcare delivery now and in the future.

Given the many obstacles in the way of implementing these technologies on a large scale in the delivery of health services, it is important that we should not relent in our efforts at promoting their widespread diffusion even in the face of these challenges. As we have noted throughout this book, and indeed, is the reason for its title, doctors must lead the way in the large-scale adoption of these technologies in the health industry. We hope that by reading this book, some of them would have made up their minds to do precisely that.

www.ingramcontent.com/pod-product-compliance
Lightning Source LLC
LaVergne TN
LVHW041217050326
832903LV00021B/665